KEEP AUSTIN WEIRD
A Guide to the Odd Side of Town
Red Wassenich

Photography by
the Author & Karen Pavelka
Illustrations by C. Thresher

Dedication

To my wife, Karen Pavelka, who is the good kind of weird.

Designed by John P. Cheek
Cover design by Bruce Waters
Type set in Impress BT/Humanist 521 BT

ISBN: 978-0-7643-2639-4
Printed in China

Schiffer Books are available at special discounts for bulk purchases for sales promotions or premiums. Special editions, including personalized covers, corporate imprints, and excerpts can be created in large quantities for special needs. For more information contact the publisher:

Published by Schiffer Publishing Ltd.
4880 Lower Valley Road
Atglen, PA 19310
Phone: (610) 593-1777; Fax: (610) 593-2002
E-mail: Info@schifferbooks.com

For the largest selection of fine reference books on this and related subjects, please visit our web site at: www.schifferbooks.com We are always looking for people to write books on new and related subjects. If you have an idea for a book please contact us at the above address.

This book may be purchased from the publisher. Include $5.00 for shipping. Please try your bookstore first. You may write for a free catalog.

In Europe, Schiffer books are distributed by
Bushwood Books
6 Marksbury Ave.
Kew Gardens
Surrey TW9 4JF England
Phone: 44 (0) 20 8392 8585; Fax: 44 (0) 20 8392 9876
E-mail: info@bushwoodbooks.co.uk
Website: www.bushwoodbooks.co.uk

Contents

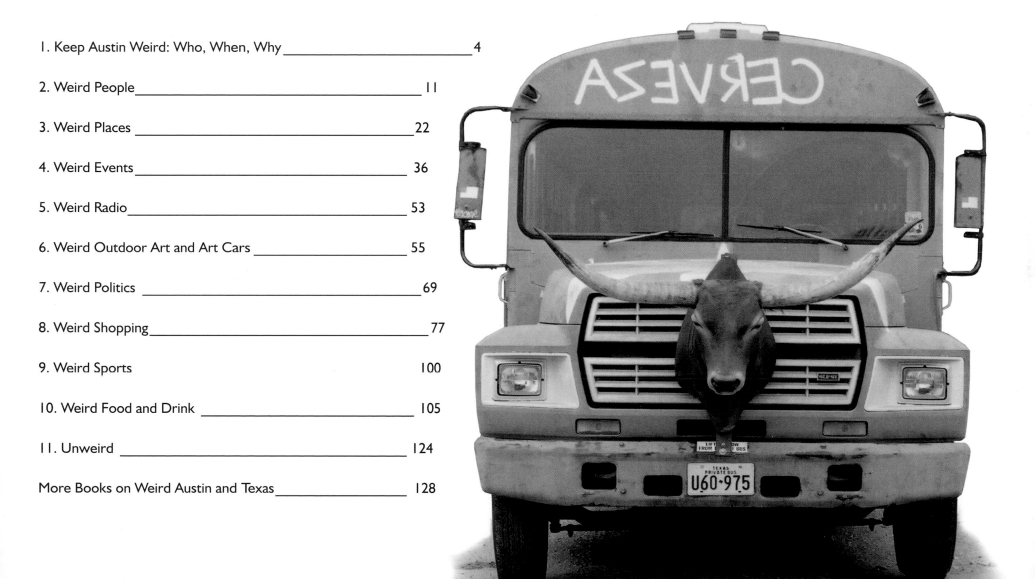

Chapter 1
Keep Austin Weird: Who, When, Why

"Keep Austin Weird" came into this world on a spring Saturday in 2000, one of the underreported consequences of Y2K. I was calling in my donation to a fund-raiser on all-volunteer radio station KOOP for *The Lounge Show*, which features smooth crooners such as Bobby Darin and Louis Prima, along with strange tunes such as Bing Crosby's "Hey Jude" and William Shatner's "Lucy in the Sky with Diamonds." When asked why I chose this show, the words came out: "It helps keep Austin weird."

Bingo. Sounds like a good slogan, I thought. I mentioned the phrase to my wife, Karen Pavelka, who soon had a thousand bumper stickers in hand. We started handing them out for free to friends and those who seemed worthy (not a mutually exclusive group). For instance, an early one went at Spamarama to the winner of the "Spam Cram," a competition to eat a can of the delicious potted meat the fastest.

Soon I had a website (www.keepaustinweird.com) up and the phrase very slowly caught on. We never tried to make money on it and have been very successful at that. Those who started giving away and selling KAW-related stuff are largely responsible for the slogan's popularity, which has some drearily ironic aspects in that the commercialization of the phrase—it's largely seen as a marketing slogan—contradicts one of our underlying inspirations for Keep Austin Weird. We wanted to stop the obsession with money and development that leads to the homogenization that makes every American city look alike. Now, some say, the phrase is becoming so widespread as to be homogenizing itself. And its use as a marketing tool is spreading to other cities, to further the irony.

As many have pointed out, the phrase Keep Austin Weird has a slightly negative nostalgia to it. If we have to make this plea, that means the battle is being lost. Sadly, that's correct.

Jim Shahin, former writer for the weekly alternative paper, the *Austin Chronicle*, described the movement thusly: "No wonder people want to KEEP AUSTIN WEIRD. A desperate plea from a distraught populace, the slogan articulates a palpable sense that Austin is losing something even more fundamental to its identity than its clean water, which, after all, can be repaired. ... The fear is that the city is losing its very identity."

But that's a different story—one that neither you nor I want to read. This book is meant to glorify the unique, screwy people, places, events, and things that keep Austin on the good side of odd; so morose whining, as much fun as that is, about how great things used to be will be kept to a minimum. Only this chapter even delves into remotely "serious" aspects of KAW.

"Weird" has many shades of meaning, from goofy to unpleasant; the latter will not be explored much (although there is an Unweird chapter herein). For instance, Austin ushered in the era of random mass sniper murders when Charles Whitman killed thirteen in 1966, shooting from the University of Texas tower. Let us instead look to the fact that Austin has the largest urban bat colony in the world.

Many, probably most, think of the weird aspects of Austin as the highly visible ones—Leslie, the cross-dressing homeless perennial mayoral candidate, funky stores along South Congress, and the freakish number of live music venues. And these are all cool, but to me the fundamental weirdness is the high quotient of everyday weirdos working in the next cubicle, living next door, sitting next to you right now, building statues out of beer bottles.

One of my next-door neighbors is a sixty-ish woman whose father built her house (and mine) in the 1930s. She moved back home after living in India for several years. The neighbors on the other side live in a large two-story house that can be difficult to walk through due to the vast collection of excellent garage sale-procured art, books, records, clothes, et cetera. Across the street is a woman in her late sixties who sings in cabarets. Behind me is a man who plays drums in a gospel group that has been going since 1949 and who puts up the best Christmas lights in town (see the Weird Events chapter). This is the substratum of weirdness upon which the mighty fortresses of oddness are built. This walking-down-the-street weirdness is harder to document, but we shall try, because that is fundamentally what Austin weird is.

Austin is quantifiably different. Psychedelic rock developed here to some degree in the mid-1960s, with the 13th Floor Elevators. Janis Joplin cut her teeth as a performer here before moving on to the West Coast. Underground comic artist Gilbert Shelton, creator of "Wonder Wart Hog" and "The Fabulous Furry Freak Brothers," started here. Outlaw country music, largely inspired by sometimes Austinite Willie Nelson, flourished in the early 1970s, with the legendary Armadillo World Headquarters (along with many other venues) showcasing it. As you can see, much of this weirdness happened decades ago. It created an aura that exists to this day, that draws would-be weirdoes who in turn pass along this mentality to the next generation, thus turning the great wheel of life a little closer to the jolly abyss.

As Keep Austin Weird has gained in popularity, gangs have formed. Here two rival groups in their colors roam downtown. Sometimes pie and seltzer fights break out as they accuse each other of being normal.

While the phrase Keep Austin Weird was invented in 2000, it didn't become a common catchphrase for a couple of years. Perhaps the main incident that popularized it was its use in a campaign by two locally owned excellent central city businesses, BookPeople and Waterloo Records, to fight a $2.1 million incentive package from the city for a developer to build a shopping center that was to include a Borders Books, right across the street from BookPeople. Steve Bercu of BookPeople and John Kunz of nearby Waterloo Records had bumper stickers printed saying "Keep Austin Weird: Support Local Businesses." They put them out for free in their stores and the fuse was lit. The bumper stickers were everywhere. Public support for their campaign grew and eventually the city backed away from the incentive and Borders backed out of the deal and stayed in the 'burbs.

A fledgling Austin Independent Business Alliance that had a few dozen members grew to its current 450. Over 155,000 bumper stickers have been given away since then.

Another byproduct of this campaign was that Steve Bercu took the support-local-businesses sermon on the road, and several cities, led by independent bookstores, have now adopted the phrase or variations. There are now at least the following Keep wherever Weird campaigns:

Keep Santa Cruz Weird
Keep Boulder Weird
Keep Louisville Weird
Keep Clarendon Weird
Keep Portland Weird

Steve Bercu of BookPeople has spread the power of weirdness throughout the country based on its use in promoting local businesses.

It's at this point I must report that evidently the phrase Keep Erie Weird was codified sometime in the 1980s. It seems to have had a short life and wasn't known by me until well after the Austin version appeared, full-blown, from my forehead. Besides, how in hell would they not go with Keep Erie Eerie?

A few cities have gone with more creative variations. Albuquerque has Keep It Querque, and for the ironists there's Keep Dallas Plastic and Keep San Antonio Lame.

More than a few people have pointed out that if all these cities are claiming weirdness, then the word has lost its meaning; weird is the new normal. Again, this use of the phrase is basically a marketing slogan for local business rather than our original whine for the preservation of goofiness; but, in the marketplace of ideas, follow the money.

The Keep Austin Weird phrase has caught on big time in Austin—it's commonly referred to as the unofficial city motto, and a Google search for the phrase gets over 70,000 hits (plus another 600 for the typo "Keep Austin Wierd")—and it has spawned many local variations. The following are "serious" enough to have bumper stickers or T-shirts.

Keep Austin Wired (various coffee shops)

Keep Austin Unwired and Keep Austin Wireless (promoting wireless internet access)

Keep Austin Free (against the ban on smoking in all public places, including bars)

Keep Austin Reading (the public library's promotional program)

Keep Austin Writing

Keep Austin Punk

Keep Austin Wild

Keep Austin Birding

Keep Austin Blue (to maintain the Democratic Party majority)

Keep Austin Planned (from Planned Parenthood)

Keep Austin Pets Weird

Keep Austin Whiskered (in support of cat animal shelters)

Keep Austin Neutered

Keep Austin Dry Cleaned (perhaps the oddest one)

Keep Austin Blind (this strange one was on a T-shirt worn by a blind teen who was learning to walk with a white cane)

A suitably odd bit of publicity for Keep Austin Weird came in December 2002 when both the *Austin American-Statesman* and the *New York Times* ran articles about a trademark dispute over the phrase. A local company applied for trademark rights to use it on hats and shirts. I was and am opposed to any limitation on who uses it and how it's used, so I got two delays on the approval process. Local humor columnist, John Kelso, ran an article about this, and the *Times* covered it in an article that included the statement that $50-a-glass wine tastings were becoming the norm in our decreasingly funky city.

Such national exposure brought various responses from around the country. One was a letter from a woman who was a member of a group called More Than Money, which is largely a group of wealthy do-gooders. She complimented my wife and me on fighting the commercialization of Keep Austin Weird. Then she said, "Let me buy you two a couple of wine-tasting tickets." There was a $100 bill inside.

The article also brought offers of free advice from several trademark lawyers, but the battle was abandoned due to the amount of money and energy it would take, plus there was the sheer boredom of the whole process. The bad guys got it.

There is, of course, cheap irony when a phrase meant in part to promote an open, un-materialistic way of life becomes a restricted cash cow for a few. In even cheaper irony, the trademark holders usually include "Support Local Businesses" along with "Keep Austin Weird," but every single one of their shirts, hats, koozies, mugs, et cetera is made outside the United States.

Austin Community College President Stephen Kinslow holds a "Keep Austin Community College Weird" notebook. (ACC is the author's employer but he had nothing to do with this use.)

How important, if at all, is the word *weird* to the success of the slogan? Would it have mattered if any of the following had been the original?

Keep Austin Odd
Keep Austin Bizarre
Keep Austin Strange
Keep Austin Offbeat
Keep Austin Uncanny
Keep Austin Eccentric
Keep Austin Loco
Keep Austin Nuts
Keep Austin Thesaurused

The word *weird* has a weird etymology. It comes from the Old English *wyrd*, which was a noun meaning fate or destiny, mainly in a supernatural sense. Its use as an adjective seems to have its earliest usage as "weird sisters," also known as three fates or Norns in Germanic mythology. Shakespeare employed this myth in *Macbeth*.

There inevitably has been a backlash against Keep Austin Weird. There are two main schools of thought, for lack of a better phrase. Some say get over yourselves; you're not that weird. Others come from the get-rid-of-the-weir-does perspective.

The get-over-yourselves crowd is exemplified by the following anonymous web posting:

For me, the slogan only really works if you accept it as a doomed, romantic gesture in the face of inevitable corporation. If Austin really was weird it would be boastful and empty to proclaim it. Austin isn't weird except in pockets and any city can claim that.

The normalcy advocates are showcased at the Make Austin Normal website:

For years, Austinites have argued we should Keep Austin Weird. But that's a cliché now. The fact is, Austin is growing up and we need to snap out of denial. We can't be protectionists forever. We can only plan for the future..

Zzzz. Oops, sorry, seemed to have dozed off there for a minute.

Then there's the more splenetic versions such as this one that came to me as an anonymous postcard:

Clamoring for weirdness is to laud a form of mental illness. The Keep Austin Weird idea is, I suspect, based on the premise that conventionality stifles creativity, that it is the goofballs who enjoy life most and also do the most ultimately to advance society. Only a child can believe such sentamentalistic [sic] drivel. But then the Sixties turned America into a land of perpetual children. You are a suitable poster child.

I'll be signing posters in the lobby at the end of this book.

There is also the somehow simultaneously annoying and interesting sociological and economic analyses of the Keep Austin Weird phenomenon. The City of Austin in 2002 published a white paper called "The Intersection of Innovation, Creativity, and Quality of Life" on the future economy of our city, and one portion was referred to as the Keep Austin Weird plan, which advocated "promoting Austin as a creative and vibrant community, helping to attract and retain creative talent." One of the main writers of this report is now mayor of Austin, Will Wynn.

Much of this sort of thinking grew out of the popularity of Richard Florida's book, *The Rise of the Creative Class*, which says that cities with a high percent of people employed in creative jobs, which includes in his definition those working in the tech sector, will prosper. Cities that have open, nonjudgmental auras will attract such folk. Florida was quoted in the local daily paper as saying, "Austin's big issue is that it's growing up. It's transitioning from a rough-and-tumble honky-tonk college and music town—with all the inherent wonderfulness of that—to a real major grown-up, wealth-creating city. And with that, there has to be another step in the cultural chain."

My follow-up: Of course this prosperity brings in the conservatives, who are drawn to money like buzzards to road kill, and who will destroy the cool vibe. Thus the "keep" part of Keep Austin Weird.

Capital Metro bus tickets got in on the act.

This being a university town in many ways, it was probably inevitable that the phrase led to a Ph.D. dissertation at U.T. "Everyday Intensities: Rhetorical Theory, Composition Studies, and the Affective Field of Culture" says in its abstract, "While the Keep Austin Weird movement can be seen as a rhetorical response to the 'exigence' of city-wide overdevelopment, we can also situate the exigence's evocation within a wider context of affective ecologies comprised of ongoing processes of material experiences, stories, moods, and public feelings." Well, that sucks the fun right out of it, doesn't it?

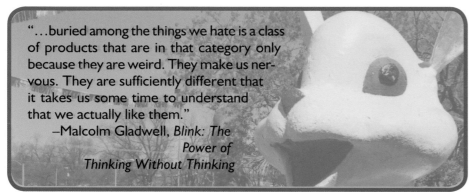

"...buried among the things we hate is a class of products that are in that category only because they are weird. They make us nervous. They are sufficiently different that it takes us some time to understand that we actually like them."
–Malcolm Gladwell, *Blink: The Power of Thinking Without Thinking*

A certain high-water mark in the institutionalization of Keep Austin Weird was the play *Keepin' It Weird* in 2005 at the Zachary Scott Theatre. This ambitious production ran for a couple of months to rave reviews in the local press. (The *Austin Chronicle* referred to it as Austin's own *Our Town*.) Dave Steakley created, wrote, and directed the three-hour production. He interviewed over 200 local weirdos and their observers, turning these into monologues and short scenes. The play tended to have perhaps a few too many observations by the non-weirdo community, such as Lady Bird Johnson, but it generally succeeded in capturing the zeitgeist.

The third act was largely devoted to the distinctly non-funny incident in 2005 when the African-American nightclub Midtown Live burned and police at the scene sent each other messages such as "Burn, baby, burn." The play explores the racial divide in Austin, which is certainly a problem, though personally, I thought the issue belonged in another play. (Many, however, thought it made the play really work.)

It does bring up the interesting topic of how much the whole Keep Austin Weird phenomenon is only white. Overwhelmingly, it seems to me, although a handful of the people and places in this book are not Anglo or are located in the "ethnic" parts of town. Of course, people of color go to Spamarama and have good yard art, and it may well just be my limited perspective, but the sorts of things celebrated herein are usually in the white community. Why is that? I hope this book will lead me to hearing more of non-Anglo weird Austin. *Mantener Austin Extraña.*

When I got the contract to write this book, I had a sinking feeling: What if Austin really isn't that weird? What if I'm just a victim of love-of-place and am living in a delusion? I'm happy to report that creating this book erased these doubts. There's a wonderful mix of knowingly weird people and things and also many traditional Texas ones that have a strange twist to them that makes them Austin. While there's plenty of evidence that the forces of homogenization are gaining ground, there is still a solid core of oddballs who are keeping Austin weird. Thank you.

It was a recurring realization as the book took shape that I was missing a million people, places, and things that should have been included. I pled with friends and experts to tell me things to include and got lots of much appreciated help, but ultimately this is largely my view of what should be included. As you look over this tome and are outraged that some art gallery that specializes in tattooed goiters wasn't included, please let me know. Send an email to keepaustinweird@keepaustinweird.com.

Even the marquee for the play behaved oddly.

The entrance to the Zach Scott Theatre was appropriately decorated for the world premiere of *Keepin' It Weird*.

Chapter 2
Weird People

Austin's weirdness, of course, all comes down to the many individual weirdoes—the blue-collar goofball who welds stuff onto his car, the artiste who paints rocks, the obsessive who collects tea cozies, the insurance agent who plays in a band and owns 150 electric guitars. We can only give a sampling here, but there is one weirdo known to all, a character so large that the local daily newspaper said he was Austin's own Mickey Mouse—Leslie Cochran.

Leslie, as he's called by all, is a middle-aged, semi-homeless cross-dresser who frequently hangs out in downtown Austin wearing a bra and thong. Oh, and he ran for mayor or city council three times, getting as much as eight percent of the vote. He's an icon for the partying crowds on 6th Street, usually surrounded by folks wanting photos and autographs or by police trying to arrest him.

In an interview, Leslie came across as a stew of off-the-chart strange, shrewd, friendly, smart, a bit lost, and as a person who, as he said, "has created his own system." He enjoys being a star. You can visit him online at www.myspace.com/44499851.

He ended up in Austin in 1996 after several years of wandering the nation by car, bicycle, and old bookmobile. He freely admits he hasn't been normal since he was in an eleven-day coma in 1977 after a motorcycle accident. As to why he has settled in Austin, he claims the reason is that soon after he first arrived he was arrested for violating the city's camping ban, aimed at the large homeless population. He was given a court date, but the police told him to just keep moving and don't bother with the court. He demurred, saying that if he left and ever returned, he'd be in deeper trouble. So he hung around for nine months, getting a not guilty verdict. But, in the meantime, he had been arrested again and the same cycle had started. He has been arrested in Austin eighty-three times, so he says it's really the Austin police—with whom, to say the least, there is not a mutual admiration society—who keep him in town as he awaits the inevitable next court date.

Leslie, the king and queen of Austin weird.

When Dave Steakley, the creator, writer, and producer of the Austin play *Keepin' It Weird*, researched the topic, he interviewed over 200 people and said the only common denominator was that everyone mentioned Leslie.

Movie stars! Swimming pools! Austin has a fairly significant film industry, with over 250 features, made-for-TV movies, and TV series shot here in the past twenty years. And a new studio is at the site of the old Mueller Airport. Along with musicians, movie folk tend to walk on the odd side of the street, helping with the weirdo demographics.

There are a couple of directors, Richard Linklater and Robert Rodriguez, who have stuck in this one-horse town despite pretty big successes. Linklater, in particular, has contributed significantly to the weirdness quotient of Austin, to which he moved in the mid-1980s. His 1991 *Slacker* is a defining archetype of the Austin weirdo lifestyle—non-materialistic, dopey, accidentally hip. His under appreciated 2001 *Waking Life* is also set in Austin, although that fact is not openly stated. It features several local oddballs, turned into animations, giving peculiar rants.

Linklater is also one of the founders of the Austin Film Society, which has grown steadily and attracted outside weirdoes to Austin, most notably, perhaps, Quentin Tarantino, who visits Austin frequently and has hosted the recurring QTFest as a fundraiser for the society since the late 1990s. Tarantino screens some of his favorite movies; many of them are obscure sleazy B horror and martial arts films. This goes on for up to ten days, and Tarantino actually attends each showing and introduces these movies retrieved from his personal archive. He is famous for insisting on these being taken seriously and for barking at snickerers and ironists.

Famous film fanatic Harry Knowles is a local who runs the website Ain't It Cool News (www.aintitcool.com), which covers the latest gossip of the film industry. Knowles has grown to wield considerable power in the industry, while remaining firmly in Austin. He hosts a yearly "Butt-Numb-A-Thon," at which he shows movies for twenty-four straight hours. These vary from vintage obscure films to the world premiere of Mel Gibson's *The Passion of the Christ*. Tarantino usually attends this event too.

Almost all these events revolve around the downtown Alamo Drafthouse. Founded by Tim and Karrie League, the Drafthouse is one of the landmarks of Austin weirdness and is highly recommended. (There are three more Drafthouses in Austin and all have some unusual events, but the original downtown location is way stranger than the others, and the only one still owned and run by the founders, who sold the others.) It opened in 1997 as an innovative combination theater, restaurant, and bar. Every other row was replaced with long tables, and waiters glide among the crowd delivering food and drinks while viewers see some truly odd movies.

Notable Alamo features: Weird Wednesdays feature a free showing of some forgotten oddity. "Foleyvision" movies are occasional films where live actors, musicians, and sound effects artists (Foley artists) are substituted for the soundtracks of such bizarre movies as *Santo vs. the Martians*, in which Mexican masked wrestlers fight invading aliens, and a low budget Turkish version of *Star Wars*. "Food and Film" pairs a film and the menu, such as *Godzilla* with sushi and sake or a spaghetti western with spaghetti. In 2005 the Alamo undertook their first "Rolling Roadshow," covering 6,000 miles in twenty-one days to show eleven films in the sites where the movie was set or shot, including *Close Encounters of the Third Kind* at Devil's Tower, Wyoming (the showing included a mashed potato sculpture contest); *North by Northwest* in the California field where the crop duster menaced Cary Grant (this showing featured crop duster flybys); *Bullit* in San Francisco (included a race through the streets before the showing); and *It Came from Outer Space* (in 3-D) in Roswell, New Mexico. A second, more ambitious roadshow was announced in summer 2006, with stops such as the actual prison for *Escape from Alcatraz*.

The Leagues, the owners, are exploring becoming a nonprofit organization as a way to lessen the horrendous downtown rental costs. Using a cool campaign based on the "real" Alamo, they are trying to save this bastion of weirdness. Please, God, don't let the Alamo go away. www.originalalamo.com.

Another Austin show biz figure from the stranger side of the mainstream is Mike Judge, creator of the TV series *Beavis and Butthead* and *King of the Hill*. Both series are set in Texas, and *King of the Hill*'s Arlen, Texas, is partially based on the working-class parts of Austin.

Austin seems to have an inordinate number of folks who obsess on collecting things, although this substratum of people dedicated to bottle caps and odd-shaped potatoes seems to exist everywhere. Often by their very nature these are obscure stashes, unavailable to those outside the collector's circle of similar obsessives, and thus difficult to document. And perhaps there isn't too much point in highlighting them because you, the curious civilian, often won't get to see these private holdings. Why taunt you with the knowledge of a cat whisker collection when you'll never get to see it?

Austin has many obsessive collectors. *Drawing by C. Thresher.*

Your author must admit to symptoms of this illness. Bowling kitsch, golf kitsch, wooden moons, and—my best collection—flattened kitchenware take up much space in my home.

Given Austin's fondness for music, it's not surprising many collectors tend toward that area. Our semiannual Austin Record Convention is the largest in the United States, filling a 50,000 square-foot space.

A record collector I know said that years ago he was sharing a house in Austin with another fanatic and their refrigerator went out one morning. By the afternoon, the fridge was filled with old records.

The author owns six wooden moons.

Some of the author's collection of mounted flattened kitchen objects come from as far away as Turkey.

Austin isn't only rock and roll. There are a number of classical music fanatics, and even these can't seem to avoid the weird side of life. A notable collector about town is Karl Miller, a librarian at the University of Texas who has dedicated one entire bedroom and much of his den and garage to his collection of recordings. He has over 10,000 and meticulously catalogs them. Karl is a serious musicologist, especially of classical music, but his collection also includes many idiosyncratic divisions, including: a "Music for…" collection, such as "Music for Robots" and "Music for Breaking Your Lease;" '50s cheesecake album covers (with a special Jayne Mansfield subcategory); 300 separate "101 Strings" albums; a "tarnished artists" collection that includes Tammy Faye Baker and Jimmy Swaggart albums; and many more.

Karl has founded a record label, Pierian, to reissue music, mainly classical and early twentieth century popular music. Several of Pierian's CDs are "The Caswell Collection," which are "reproducing piano rolls," much superior to the normal piano rolls most of us schlubs are familiar with. These reproduce famous pianists and composers from days of yore actually playing, using a complex system combining how the rolls are marked and the pumps inside the piano.

Record collector Karl Miller displays some of his Jayne Mansfield gems.

Ken Caswell owns two reproducing piano-roll players. These Rube Goldbergian devices recreate famous pianists actually performing.

These come from the collection of Ken Caswell, a genial gentleman from an old Austin family. (Locals are likely familiar with the beautiful Caswell House at West Avenue and 15th Street.) Ken has a pair of rare reproducing pianos that perform the songs. It's an interesting experience to sit in his living room and listen to a long-dead pianist play "live."

Another esoteric collection comes from Jim Cartwright, who owns dozens of antique phonographs, including some of the earliest Edison machines. His west Austin home is stuffed with bizarre and beautiful machines and records. He is an encyclopedia of recording history, both on the devices and the music itself. His business, Immortal Performances, sells phonographs and records at the Old Time Treasures antiques mall in Round Rock and also at his home at 1404 West 30th Street.

Jim Cartwright has a huge collection of antique records and players.

A good representative of the everyday Austin weirdo collector is Penny Van Horn. By day an office drone, at other times a strange artist—with a published comic titled *Recipe for Disaster*—and a collector. Besides the collections pictured here, she also keeps hundreds of mosquitoes and fleas that she has killed and placed under tape. See some of her excellent artwork at www.pennyvanhorn.com.

Penny Van Horn with her collections of gerbil-chewed wood and cat whiskers.

Real collectors have very specific, well organized obsessions. *Drawing by C. Thresher.*

David Lee Pratt and his wife, Susan Maynard, are part of a small, amazingly funky art enclave, called Spunky Monkey Ranch at 2213-B South 1st Street. This is located behind a small set of hip shops. They owned the late, lamented Alternate Current gallery, which was in this odd collection of stores and studios. David is a tie-dyed in the wool iconoclastic visual artist and actor and raconteur. You should drop by and check out the art at their ranch and the neighboring artists and revolutionaries. Austin should declare this area a city monument.

The grounds of the Spunky Monkey Ranch.

David Lee Pratt in the kitchen of the Spunky Monkey Ranch amidst his wife's ceramics.

John Kelso has been writing his thrice weekly observational humor column for the daily *Austin American-Statesman* since 1977, a remarkable feat in journalism. He generally looks at vaguely or blatantly stupid or pretentious people or events from the perspective of a curmudgeonly populist. Idiots like ex-Congressman Tom DeLay are perfect grist for his mill. Kelso compared DeLay to Saddam Hussein: "One guy had the Republican Guard. The other used to be the Republican guard." In another column, in March 2006, he published the results of a reader poll of least admired people. The results: George W. Bush 62 percent, Sarah (a former famously cranky waitress at the Dry Creek Cafe) 10 percent, Saddam Hussein 10 percent, Jeffrey Dahmer 5 percent, O.J Simpson 5 percent, Barry Bonds 4 percent, and Ken Lay 3 percent. In a 2006 article, Kelso advocated putting out "roach traps for Republicans."

Needless to say this sort of thing gets plenty of negative reaction from the tight-sphincter crowd. But Kelso said in an interview that the article that got the biggest reaction was not about politics. Following a column in which he professed his dislike of the Dallas Cowboys, he had over 300 messages on his answering machine, and the first one set the tone: "Why don't you move to San Fransissyco?"

Neal Pollack is the wiseass author of several books, including *The Neal Pollack Anthology of American Literature* and *Nevermind the Pollacks: A Rock and Roll Novel*. He writes a good blog at www.nealpollack.com.

John Kelso has been making fun of everything for three decades.

Spike Gillespie is the author of *Pissed Off: On Women and Anger* among other books. For someone interested in that topic, she's awfully jolly. She also has written for many major periodicals, does commentaries on the local NPR station, and is involved in all sorts of interesting activities, from knitting to the local music scene. Witness her antics at www.spikeg.com

There are dozens of tattoo parlors in Austin and one of the best according to many is Southside Tattoo. Karen Slafter, selected best tattoo artist by the readers of the *Austin Chronicle*, works there and is a very genial weirdo. She's also a talented painter. See her paintings and tattoos, along with others from this parlor, at www.southsidetattoo.com. 1313 S. Congress.

This friendly native has complied with the city's Mandatory Body Art law.

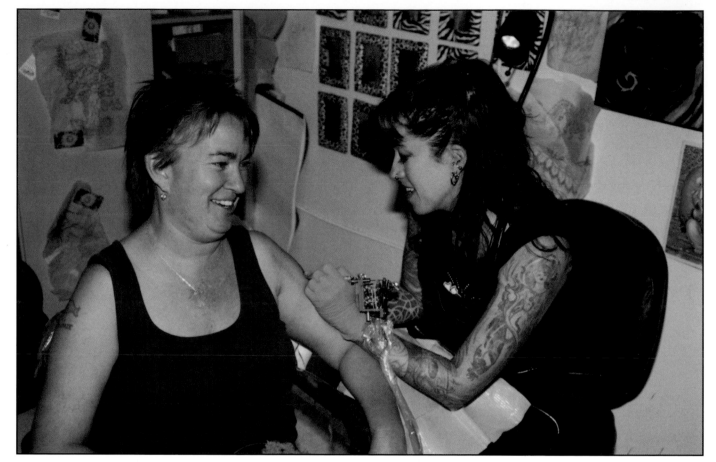

Karen Slafter of Southside Tattoo works on Austin writer Spike Gillespie.

Austin, like all modern American towns, has many tattooed and pierced denizens, but we take it really far. In 2004 the city council passed the "Mandatory Body Art" law, which requires all citizens between sixteen and sixty-five to have at least one tattoo and one piercing. All sorts of ramifications followed: Do ear piercings count? Yes. Do temporary tattoos count? No. Can one person get multiple tattoos or piercings and make up for someone who doesn't want any? This is currently working its way up the appeals courts.

Satan's Cheerleaders: Squad 666 are a fun lovin', devil worshippin' bundle of dancing energy that performs with bands, at art openings and parties, wherever. They are, as they say on their website, "quite active in the 'black' arts of Shameless Self-Promotion." Remarkably, they have been going since 1995, a testament to the underlying evil of the Austin weirdo community. www.satanscheerleaders.com

Want to brighten up your next party? Hire Satan's Cheerleaders!

Chapter 3
Weird Places

Especially if you are new to Austin, a great and unusual way to see the heart of it is to take one of the tours offered by SegCity. These are done on those ultracool Segway gliding devices that truly seem like magic. This company pushes the Keep Austin Weird angle (you can pick up a KAW hat and shirt there). You get to see Congress Avenue, 6th Street, Town Lake, the Bremond block, the Capitol, and the south edge of U.T. (the fuddy duddies there won't allow the Segways on campus), led by a friendly guide. A three-hour tour is a bit pricey at $65 but really fun and you'll be the envy of everyone you pass. 621 East 6th Street. www.segcity.com

Although there are real goofballs all over town, Austin's weirdness tends to clump. There are a handful of zones where most of the odder shopping and residential areas are. Currently south Austin (which usually refers to the area below Town Lake and west of Congress Avenue, also identified by its zip code, 78704) lays claim to being the hotspot in most people's minds. The area proudly proclaims its identity with multiple bumper stickers:

"78704: Not Just a Zip Code But a Way of Life"
"78704: Not Just a Waste of Life"
"78704Ever"
"78741: My Zip Code Can Beat Up Your Zip Code"
"South Austin: We're All Here Because We're Not All There"

There has long been a mock culture war between north and south Austin, with the former seen as the gentrified and the latter the red-necked. There used to be a great event that pitted the yuppies versus bubbas in the "Tug of Honor." Held for three years starting in 1987, this tug of war had hundreds of people on each shore of Town Lake pulling on a massive rope across at least 300 feet of water. The north squad featured white-collar professionals, artsy types, and university folks (including the occasional U.T. football player), and the south had bikers and rednecks. Refreshments on the north were brie and white wine. The southerners had hot dogs and canned beer. One year the crafty north team tied their end to a bridge and stood around sipping Chardonnay while the dimwits on the far shore wore themselves out. But to no avail—the south won every year. The event was a successful fundraiser to build a youth hostel. It was the brainchild of state representative Charlie Gandy, who also once proposed a "running of the lawyers" down Congress Avenue. Once the hostel was a reality, the tug of honor ceased. Someone needs to revive it.

The xylophone doorbell is a first clue that **Casa Neverlandia** isn't your normal south Austin home. This stunning residence sits among nice, normal, small frame houses on a quiet street, but, lord, is it different. James Talbot took a one-story 1917 beat-up house that he bought in 1979 and, later joined by his partner Kay Pils, turned it into a three-level wonderland. One of Talbot's areas of expertise is playground design, and that sense of fun suffuses the house. Multicolored mirrors line the eaves. Elaborate masonry and weaving trails of bright ceramics are everywhere. The interior also has a spectacular sense of whimsy. Inspired by Gaudi and other Spanish avant-garde architects, the couple created rooms with rounded corners and swirling abstract protrusions. Talbot's excellent works of art, mainly intricate beadwork and ceramic pieces, are both adornment and part of the house itself. There is a huge tower in back with a great view that is accessed by a scary bridge. Three fire poles around the premises allow entertaining egress. Kay's use of fabrics adds an exotic air.

Talbot and Kay are part of the fun. Friendly, droll, down-to-earth intellectuals with high skill levels in a variety of endeavors from bookkeeping to alternative energy, plus, of course, art, architecture, and carpentry, they have done the vast majority of work on Neverlandia themselves. They are very dedicated to leading environmentally low-impact lives, and their home has solar panels, rainwater collection, and—the real sacrifice in Texas—no air conditioning or central heating. (OK, there is the "sin room," with a window unit and their one TV.) This couple should run Austin.

It is their home after all, so visits to Casa Neverlandia are limited to organized groups of ten or more and a fee is charged. Contact Talbot and Kay at kaytal@io. com. A reprint of an article from the *Austin American-Statesman* on the house, including nice photos, is at www.io.com/~kaytal/casa/index.html.

Kay Pils and James Talbot, creators of Casa Neverlandia.

Far left:
The front of Casa Neverlandia.

Left:
A rear view of Neverlandia.

View from the master bedroom to the scary bridge leading to the three-story tower in back.

Interior of Neverlandia.

An example of Talbot's beautiful beaded artwork.

The **Cathedral of Junk** is something to throw in the face of anyone who questions Austin's weirdness—although its creator doesn't consider Austin weird. A work of wonder created by Vince Hannemann, a low-key visionary who started assembling this mass of interconnected stuff in 1989. It has grown to be three stories tall and bigger than Vince's 800 square foot house. Originally called Yardspace 11 because it was the eleventh outdoor art undertaking Vince has done in his life, it's kind of like a multi-room, multilevel igloo built by and of demented robots. It weighs over sixty tons and is surprisingly sturdy, held to-

The Cathedral of Junk.

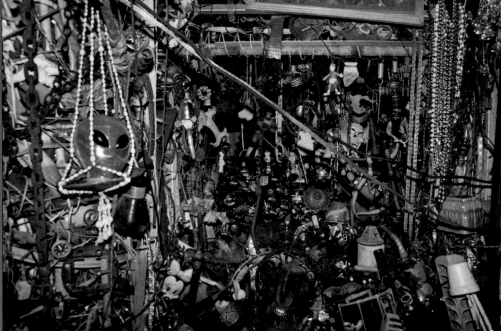

gether with lots of wire. There are objects of all kinds incorporated in it, from hubcaps to TVs to "over 700 bicycles." Vince reports his neighbors in this unassuming area south of Ben White are very cool about having this Mecca in the neighborhood, although some anonymous source once siced the city's engineers on him, but the structure was ruled sound. Vince welcomes visitors, including school groups. (Students from the School for the Blind have visited multiple times, and Vince reports they fearlessly scrambled all over it.) He holds open houses on Saturday evenings and during the day on Sunday, but it doesn't hurt to call and confirm. Donations encouraged. 512-299-7413. 4422 Lareina Drive. There's a nice article on the Cathedral on the Roadside America website: www.roadsideamerica. com/attract/TXAUSjunk.html

A detail from the Cathedral of Junk. Amazingly, this amount of junk is all solidly built.

The genius behind the Cathedral of Junk, Vince Hannemann, stands amid his creation while musicians perform "MachineMemesis"—"a nuclear fusion of sci-fi junk jazz, industrio-hillbilly chamber music, and disembodied voices from two centuries of high technology"—a collaboration with the Museum of Natural and Artificial Ephemerata.

Smut Putt Heaven is a phrase that no doubt conjures a Freudian stew of images in each person's head. That's the name of the south Austin backyard creation of Scott Stevens, which he started in 1995. His business card describes him as a "yardist," and this combination of cacti, life-sized doll heads, bottles, plastic lids, and other castoffs creates an oddly dissonant feel of peaceful garden and nightmare. Scott, a friendly, well-spoken guy, says the music of Alice Cooper is one inspiration. He and his wife collect the heads from beauty schools, where the students hack at them. The name, Smut Putt, comes from a comic book Scott created when he was a kid. He added Heaven both because he feels it has that quality (he and his wife were married in the backyard) and to tie in with the nearby Cathedral of Junk. The two creators are good friends. Like the Cathedral's creator, Scott does not consider Austin weird. It must have something to do with being on the inside looking out if two creators of major weirdo places don't see Austin as weird. Compared to their inner visions, it doesn't live up, I suppose. Call or e-mail to visit. Donations accepted. 444-1239. kickapoo23@hotmail.com

Scott Stevens, creator of Smut Putt Heaven.

A vista of Smut Putt Heaven.

When the Blanton Museum of Art opened in April 2006, the common response was, "At last, finally, Austin has a real museum." Thus is displayed ignorance of the **Museum of Natural and Artificial Ephemerata** ("where you have been all along"), a wonderful collection of eccentric objects gathered by eccentrics for eccentrics. Scott Webel and Jen Hirt operate this small but potent tribute to "miraculous traces, singular events, hypnogogica, petrifications, and taxidermied beasts: a still life where only eddies of dust express movement." The core of the collection comes from Webel's great grandparents, who founded the museum in Tucson, Arizona, in 1921. After their demise, the objects were boxed up and undiscovered until 1999. The museum was re-established and moved to Austin in 2001. Divided into the Machine Arcade and the Impermanent Collection, the museum is an exploration of the stuff of life that usually is ignored but that is actually extremely influential.

Jen Hirt and Scott Webel operate the Museum of Natural and Artificial Ephemerata in east Austin. Here at an opening of a new show, they hold a cake that was composed entirely of genetically modified ingredients.

The Machine Arcade includes such items as three containers of invisible-to-the-eye nanotechnology, two examples of 1950s no-work weight reduction machines, an orgone accumulator, a psychedelic art object one observes with eyes closed (Webel thinks this may be unique in the visual art world), a scrap of canvas from the world's largest painting (three miles wide, done by Jon Banvard, in the nineteenth century, later cut up into pieces as theater curtains), and many other thought-provoking items.

A variety of technological wonders from the Machine Arcade in the museum, including a theremin (lower right) and a cylindrical psychedelic light machine that one observes with eyes closed.

The Impermanent Collection, which "demonstrates the most advanced methods for the reproduction of absence," is an eclectic conglomeration of this and that. A stuffed jackalope; a lock of Elvis's hair; rivets from the very first Ferris wheel built for the 1893 Columbian Exhibition in Chicago (the Ferris wheel was the very first machine built for the purposes of pleasure rather than work, according to curator Hirt); and a Jolly Rancher given to the museum owners by David Hasselhoff, star of *Baywatch*, are a sample of the objects of fascination.

The Impermanent Collection of the Museum of Ephemerata.

The curators also brew Doc Chowder's Revivifying Tonic, "healthy home-brew kombucha tea!" This frightening nonalcoholic fermented drink, made from giant mushrooms, is supposed to have a variety of health benefits (and threats). According to the museum's website, Webel and Hirt suspect kombucha may have extraterrestrial origins and that the leftovers after fermentation may be a substitute for leather.

The Museum of Ephemerata has occasional special exhibits. For example, on May 6, 2006, they paid tribute to the 111th anniversary of Austin's Moonlight Towers (see below). Live music, commemorative T-shirts, and a birthday cake made with only genetically altered ingredients highlighted the celebration. Their excellent website includes directions and visiting hours—Saturdays, 12 – 3 as of this writing. 1808 Singleton Ave. www.mnae.org

Doc Chowder's Revivifying Tonic kombucha tea fermenting at the Museum of Ephemerata.

The **Moonlight Towers** are relics from the 1890s (May 6, 1895, to be exact). The 165-foot tall iron structures represented the state of the art in urban lighting. Austin's, in fact, were purchased used from Detroit. Originally there were thirty-one around what is now central Austin, and seventeen remain, the only active ones left in the U.S. Until the 1920s, each one had to be lit by hand every night by a worker who took a mini-elevator that is in the center of the structures. Growing up, I was taught to call them Freshman Moons by my father, who said that in the 1930s, when he was at U.T., they would try to convince gullible new students from the sticks that the light came from the moon. We also were told the towers were placed in the shape of a star when viewed from above, but that evidently isn't true. According to *Ripley's Believe It or Not*, in 1930, an eleven-year-old named Jimmie Fowler fell from the top of one of the towers, bouncing down the side. He awoke from a coma nine days later with 187 stitches. He grew up to be famous Austin rock guitarist Jimmie Vaughan. Today these relics (the towers, not Jimmie Vaughan) are on the National Register of Historic Places.

In an example of mass hysteria, every night from spring to fall over 1.5 million Austinites go to the Congress Avenue bridge and worship the statue of a **bat** pictured below. Evidently they seem to believe in its magical power to drive away mosquitoes. www.batcon.org

The lone
Austin bat.

The area from Guadalupe to Duval and 38th to 45th Streets comprises **Hyde Park**. Given that this is considered very much an inner-city neighborhood, it's a sign of how fast Austin has grown that it wasn't even in the city limits until the 1930s. Now it's a very pleasant, very expensive area. There are some gorgeous Victorian homes and still some humble shacks, with the latter on the endangered list. Hyde Park is too pleasant somehow to bring out the hardcore weirdoes of neighborhoods like 78704, but it has its moments, such as the annual Christmas frenzy on 37th Street (see Weird Events section).

The schizo quality of Hyde Park. Beautiful, sometimes eccentric, old houses and funky student hovels.

The shopping area around Duval and 43rd Street is a nice area to hang out and watch the natives go by. There's Quakenbush's Bakery and Julio's Restaurant and other eateries that draw the bohemian crowd. Take a stroll down any of the shady streets and you'll run into some beautiful homes, some goofy yard art, and the people who love them.

The Avenue B Grocery (4403 Avenue B) is an eccentric, old school business amidst the gentrification of Hyde Park. They make excellent sandwiches.

Another old central Austin neighborhood with an interesting history, and that is home to a higher than average number of oddballs (including your humble author), is the area commonly known as **Clarksville**. Technically, Clarksville is a small area within the Old West Austin neighborhood, but the former name is often applied to this area west of Lamar to MoPac and from Enfield Road to Town Lake. The official Clarksville has (barely these days) a small pocket of African Americans in a town that is quite segregated (Anglos in the west, Blacks and Hispanics in the east). Clarksville was founded after the Civil War when freed slaves moved from the nearby Pease plantation and set up their own village. Remarkably, amid the growth of Austin and despite municipal disregard or antagonism, it maintained well until the late twentieth century. (The streets weren't paved until the mid-1970s, and the building of the MoPac highway wiped out a third of the neighborhood.) Today only a handful of African American families remain, and the general area is being scarred by rampant gentrification. Charming but humble cottages are being replaced by gargantuan lot-filling mansions, a common practice throughout the older sections of Austin. But the area is still a treasure of illogical street design and funky houses and recently was placed on the National Register of Historic Places. It has been said it has the most liberal voting precincts in the state.

The **Santa Rita oil well** at the corner of San Jacinto and Martin Luther King Boulevard is a reconstructed rig that's a tribute to the source of much of the University of Texas's endowment. In my well-misspent college days, a reliable gag was to take some stoned newbies by it late at night and watch them lose it when the well started talking. Every few minutes a sonorous voice tells the stirring tale of how the discovery of oil on university-owned land in West Texas let Jed Clampett get a degree in genetic engineering and create the first U.T. team to win a national championship in football.

The Haskell House in Clarksville (1703 Waterston) was built around 1875 and is typical of the homes built by the freed slaves in this enclave of African Americans in west Austin. Today this would sell for about $400,000. Only kidding…maybe.

The Santa Rita oil well at U.T. It speaks good English.

Amid the hideous tracts of apartment complexes around East Riverside Drive stands an oddity. The **Metropolis Apartments** actively markets itself as being for artsy weirdoes. Unusual exterior designs on each building shout out their demographic, and amenities include complementary weekend raves. Also it's built and operated on eco-friendly standards. 2308 S. Pleasant Valley.

A grande dame of Austin's offbeat art world is **Esther's Follies**. Since 1977 this neo-Vaudeville revue has been playing on 6th Street. Satire, magic, singing, juggling, acrobatics, all with an Austin twang. It even includes pedestrians passing by the large windows behind the stage into the show. Cofounders Shannon Sedwick and Michael Shelton still produce and perform. 525 East 6th Street. www.esthersfollies.com

The Metropolis Apartments actively seek weirdo tenants.

A tribute to Austin's up-and-down tech economy is the **Intel Building**. Located prominently downtown on West 5th, this shell was left in 2001 when the chip maker's bottom line started smelling like a bottom. Aside from being the setting for an avant-garde dance piece in 2006, it has just been an eyesore. There are plans to tear it down and build a new federal courthouse on the site, but the teardown alone will cost $3 million. I say it should be used as a multistory driving range.

How often is there an assassination attempt on a tree? Austin's **Treaty Oak** suffered that fate in 1989. A bad kind of weirdo poisoned the huge 500-year-old live oak with an herbicide in an attempt to cast a spell. A huge rescue effort was undertaken, with Ross Perot paying for much of it. Amazingly the tree survived, although over half of it died, leaving what was once described by the American Forestry Association as the most perfect tree in North America as a lopsided symbol of something or the other. The moron who did the deed got nine years in the slammer, where he spent his time whittling. Baylor Street, between 5th and 6th Streets

Esther's Follies has been a mainstay in Austin's performing arts scene since the 1970s.

Chapter 4
Weird Events

Austinites like to gather and act odd. The are hundreds of one-time events every year that easily fall into the weird category, but here are listed the impressive number of recurring goofy events, roughly in chronological order. For the one-time ones, the best way to keep up with them is the calendar section of the *Austin Chronicle* or a website/blog like www.austinist.com.

Carnaval Brasileiro is an annual revelry with sweaty sambas and skimpy outfits. It has been going since 1975 when some Brazilian students at U.T. held a party at the local Unitarian church. Now thousands of barely dressed hedonists brave midwinter temperatures—OK, sometimes it's chilly—every February. The posters promoting the event are always a treat. See a gallery of them and get more info at www.carnavalaustin.com.

Even something as happy-faced as a kite festival becomes somewhat weird just by the obsessiveness of the participants and the size of the crowd. Over 25,000 attend the **Zilker Kite Festival**, which began in 1929 when a fat cat who had lost it all in the stock market crash tried to hang himself by tying a string around his neck and launching a kite made from worthless stock certificates. The festival is held in March at Zilker Park. www.zilkerkitefestival.com

Valentine's Day means monkey love.

Spring Break means the **South by Southwest Music Festival** in Austin. This behemoth has grown into a nine-day event that includes interactive media and film festivals on top of the frightening number of music groups that play from Wednesday to Sunday. SXSW began in 1987 with a modest 700 attendees. By 2006 there were 10,000 attendees and 1,300 bands from all over the world playing in over sixty venues. As with so many things in Austin, natives argue whether success has ruined it. What was once a cheap, mainly local festival is now a bit pricey and very crowded. Is that progress? Whatever one feels about SXSW, there's a definite buzz in town the whole week. The downtown streets are clogged with blackened hipsters, getting blearier by the day. www.sxsw.com

The South by Southwest Music Festival crowds the streets with out of town weirdoes, guitars strapped to their backs, marching down South Congress.

SXSW attracts exotic musicians from the world over. *Drawing by C. Thresher.*

Music fanatics, techno nerds, and assorted mutants fill the streets during South by Southwest. *Drawing by C. Thresher.*

Spamarama is arguably the premier weirdo event on the annual calendar. This tribute to the potted meat has been going since 1976 when David Dryden Arnsberger and John Booher came up with the idea as a spit in the eye of the overdone chili cook-offs that are rife in Texas. Success ensued. The event has become a bit too normal, with lots of booths selling crud, but at its heart—the cook-off—it is still great. Cooks compete in the gourmet or insane categories. My all time favorite in the latter category was an operating room theme. A mannequin was stretched out with its lower abdomen cut open. Inside was ground up, slightly greenish Spam that the long line of tasters dipped out with chips. Yum. In addition to the cook-off, there's the Spam Cram eating contest. A Weimaraner once finished first easily but broke the rule that you have to keep it down for over ninety seconds. Spamarama is a fundraiser for Disability Assistance of Central Texas, so you can feel good about eating that gelatinous pink gunk. Spamarama is held in the first week of April in Waterloo Park. www. spamarama.org

At Spamarama a genial gent who served shots of Spambalaya matched each taker. It was darn good actually.

Did you know there is a Spam Museum in Austin? Sadly it's in Austin, Minnesota, the home of Hormel and Spam. I have this fantasy of a bunch of confused suits in Austin, Minnesota, sitting around a conference table in April studying sales graphs on which there's this huge spike in the other Austin. The museum claims, among other things, that Spam was stolen from hunters by Bigfoot and that Spam has been to the top of Mount Everest. It even has a tape loop of Monty Python's Spam skit. What hath irony wrought?

Food for weird gods. Spambrosia was skewers of Spam and pineapple dipped in a chocolate fountain.

In the gourmet category, this elegant presentation almost hid the fact it's still Spam.

The Sowpremes entertain the masses at Spamarama.

Who could resist Spam sushi? Me.

Four blocks north of Spamarama occurs another gourmet event, the **Edible Book Festival**. This is actually an international event that began in 2000 and is now celebrated in over sixteen countries and dozens of cities on April 1. Austin's version has been going since 2003 and is organized by those wacky students in the Kilgarlin Center for Preservation of the Cultural Record at the U.T. School of Information. The "books" have to be entirely made from edible stuff, but entries stretch that with treats such as 20,000 Leeks Under the Sea, made of leeks under blue-green Jell-O. Even bookworms crawl away. Held April 1 at the corner of M.L. King Avenue and Red River Street. The local festival's website is www.ischool.utexas. edu/~ebf/ and the international one is www.books2eat.com.

Edible Book Festival entries.

A Day in the Life

Spring brings out the weirdo events in force. On April 1, 2006, there were simultaneously Spamarama; The Edible Book Festival; The Austin Arts Festival, which isn't particularly weird but this year the guests were conceptual artists Christo and Jeanne-Claude; the Lone Star Rod & Kustom Round Up, which features lots of cool cars and rockabilly; Art Outside, the strange art show in a vacant part of South Austin; the Austin Record Convention, the largest such event in the country; and an eighteenth birthday party for Homer the Homeless Goose. For doubters of Austin's weirdness, try hitting all those.

Art Outside began in 2005 and happens for two weekends in March and April normally. That is the only normal thing about it. It is a bizarre collection of artists, both polished and rough, displaying their work and performing in an odd three-acre area off West Oltorf, near Lamar. The Enchanted Forest was listed as a hobo encampment as late as the 1970s, and it does have a different vibe, especially when filled with works by 200 artists. By night it's especially strange, and the music supposedly goes to dawn. "Brought to you by Artists for a Work-Free America." 1404 West Oltorf. www.myspace. com/artoutside and www.artoutside.org

Art Outside featured inventive works such as these.

Eeyore's Birthday Party is one of the most famous of the city's silly gatherings. It began in 1963 as a picnic in honor of the woeful donkey from *Winnie-the-Pooh,* then into essentially a keg party for the U.T. English Department. A couple of hundred students and faculty drank beer in Eastwoods Park. There was a live donkey, and the only costume was on a professor, also in a donkey suit. The live donkey remains, but otherwise it has grown into a massive, free, all day party, with a crowd of up to 20,000, many in costumes, many stoned. Although seen as a celebration of Austin's hippie past (and present), there are lots of activities for children too. One of the signature aspects of Eeyore's involves the drum circles. Hundreds of people beat on every kind of drum for at least eight continuous hours, wreathed in illegal smoke, while sometimes scantily clad Dionysians writhe in (or on) ecstasy, caught up in a haze of purple prose. Held the last Saturday in April in Pease Park. eeyores.sexton.com

Eeyore's Birthday Party…those drums. They drive the natives wild.

Nothing celebrates a beloved children's story better than a guy in buttless leather pants blowing bubbles.

Eeyore's brings out
the family-oriented
folks too.

Old hippies never die.
They go to Eeyore's.

A largely unknown treasure in Austin is **Barsana Dham**. This Hindu temple is in a (as of this moment) largely undeveloped portion of southwest Austin, off of Highway 1826. Built on a beautiful 200-acre property, the temple was constructed by craftsman imported from India. In the spring, *Mela*, an open house and festival, is held, with interesting variations on the usual events one expects at a church fair. In addition to pony rides, there are elephant rides; in addition to snow cones, there is masala dosa; in addition to T-shirts for sale, there are saris. Largely due to the high tech sector in Austin, there is a thriving Indian community, and many show up in their native finery. Their flashy website also shows the techie influence, with the cursor showering flower petals. www.barsanadham.org

Forget graduation, forget the U.T. baseball team inevitably winning conference, forget the annual flood. May means only one thing to Austin—puns. Since 1977, the annual **O. Henry Pun-off World Championship** brings the city to a standstill. Actually it is remarkably popular, with several hundred fans watching dozens of punsters competing for cheesy trophies. The event is held on the downtown grounds of the O. Henry Museum. The author of many famous and mediocre short stories was an Austin native and coined one of the city's nicknames, "The City of the Violet Crown," which appeared in 1894 in the story "Tictocq" in the newspaper he founded, *The Rolling Stone*. That's all true and there are no puns in this paragraph. You're welcome. www.punpunpun.com

Just to get a taste of the extraordinary range of off-center events in Austin, here's a tiny sample from one events listing in the *Austin Chronicle* covering a couple of weeks:

Sogkran Festival (Thai/Cambodian/Laotian new year)
Curiosities of the Nanotechnological Era, at the Museum of Natural and Artificial Ephemerata
Griffin School Re-Prom, a chance for the over-the-hill to try to do the high school prom right this time
Eat a Grilled Green Chile Pork Enchilada, for charity
Hill Country Nudists Introductory Meeting
Traditional Mayan Calendar Study
Central Texas Accordion Society
Balinese Kecak (Monkey Chant)

Late spring brings a constant guttural roar the weekend of the **Republic of Texas Biker Rally** (or ROT Rally, as they proudly call it). This really noisy and smelly event is huge and turns Austin's image as a bohemian arty place on its head as thousands of large hairy bikers and the men who love them fill the streets. The 2006 parade down Congress Avenue set the Guinness record for "Largest Parade of Motorcycles." www.rotrally.com

Austin has a ridiculous number of foot races, triathlons, and other forms of self-torture. Almost every weekend some major roadway is closed and peopled by grim, haggard, sweating drivers shooting the finger at the jolly, healthy runners. One annual event that originated in Austin in 2002 and has spread to other cities is the **Urban Assault Race**. It's a mix of biking, mental challenges, acting out scenes, and dopey tasks such as riding a giant rubber ducky in Town Lake or hunting rubber snakes in a vat of suds. Pairs compete together and can do the course in any sequence they choose. Yea for anarchy! Held in June. www.urbanassaultrace.com

More racing news: In the spring there's the Capitol 10,000, the largest 10K in Texas, and late summer or fall brings the **Keep Austin Weird 5K**. Entrants are encouraged to dress abnormally. This race is sponsored by the company that makes most of the Keep Austin Weird gimcracks and novelty items. It suffered a major setback in 2006 when they accidentally printed shirts and registration forms for the race that called it the "Keep Austin Weird 5000K." That comes out to over 3,100 miles. A city judge ruled that the contestants were indeed required to run that far. Over 700 people died in what turned into a nightmare twelve-day slog in blistering heat. Many people sued, of course, and the sponsoring company was put out of business.

Just as the "hipoisie" are getting over their six-month hangover from South by Southwest, **Austin City Limits Festival** comes around in September. ACL Fest is a spinoff of the long-running PBS TV series. This three-day event held outdoors in Zilker Park has over 130 bands on multiple stages and draws 70,000 per day, many of them weird. One day during the event in 2005 the temperature hit 108. You could bake your marijuana brownies on the sidewalk. www.aclfestival.com

The Austin Art Car Parade happens in the fall. Several dozen local and out-of-town odd-o-mobiles weave down Congress Avenue and gather at a lot in the hip SoCo area where spectators can check them out. It sticks in my craw that Austin isn't more of a hotbed of art cars. It just seems like a perfect fit. Go to this event and be inspired. (See some local cars in the Weird Outdoor Art and Art Cars chapter.) www.austinartcar.com

Halloween is, to state the obvious, a big holiday everywhere (except in conservative Christian enclaves), but Austin takes it pretty far. Those enclaves, also known as the rest of Texas, think of Austin as a pagan roadhouse on the highway to hell, and we try to accommodate. Crowds of up to 200,000 (that's not a typo) show up to walk in circles on 6th Street, Austin's famed party district where the sidewalks are formed entirely of crusted vomit. Some excellent costumes are to be seen, including over 300 dressed in police outfits. People all over Austin decorate for Halloween almost as much as for Christmas. Something about satanic powers controlling the town, I suppose.

A Halloween salute to avian flu.

Although this is Halloween, you can see people like these most nights on 6th Street.

The true meaning of **Christmas** is the celebration of the mystery of how agitated electrons can become gaudy strings of colored lights. There are good examples of overkillowatts all over town, but the most famous is on West 37th Street, just east of Guadalupe. Since the early 1980s many neighbors have joined forces to wow the masses with both the extent and the creativity of their holiday lights. After dark for the month of December, crowds of pedestrians and a traffic jam fill the street to see programmed lights that create an erupting volcano, the back of an illuminated station wagon with small goudas in a manger celebrate "the baby cheeses," and there are always some neon menorahs and a driedel. The pièce de résistance is always the home of Jamie Lipman. He wraps his entire house in black plastic to set off the lights that form a second siding. And his real genius is the inventiveness in lights. Often he simply attaches the box of lights to the house without unstringing them. When he does unstring, he's not content with simple garlands of lights; he encases the bulbs in old prescription bottles, Tic-Tac boxes, miniature liquor bottles, and such. He wraps his outdoor electric meter, which has become a dervish, with more lights, and appreciative visitors

pin dollars on the clothesline next to it to defray the utility costs.

Several years ago, the city electric department started taking down some lights strung across the street from telephone poles, saying it was a code violation. The residents simply shut down all their lights, and an outraged populace forced the city to back down.

That said, there sadly seems to be a decline on 37th. As speculators buy up houses in the hot real estate market that is central Austin, homeowners give way to student renters, who are much less likely to participate in such quaintery. In recent years there have been fewer lights, more trash, and—another partridge in the coalmine—vendors selling crap at both ends of the street.

37th Street Christmas extravaganza. The home of Jaime Lipman is encrusted with lights.

Lipman modifies his lights using baby food jars and liquor bottles and rolling papers.

Another 37th Street front yard featured a manger scene in the oven.

The best single household Christmas display is at 1611 W. 12th Street at the home of Willis Littlefield. Willis is a genial genius when it comes to decorating, and he is usually out front in his Santa cap greeting passersby. Not only does he have tons of lights on the Clarksville house he grew up in, but he also adds many extras, including up to twenty robotic figures, usually Santa but also James Brown and Ray Charles. There's always music playing from his light-show speakers, often that of the gospel group Willis is the drummer and manager for, The Bells of Joy (who have been going since the 1940s and had a number-one hit with "Let's Talk About Jesus" in the 1950s).

Willis Littlefield stands amidst his wonderful Christmas décor, including his twenty robotic figures.

Willis's Christmas visions dance with flamingoes and angels.

First Night is an all-day New Year's Eve collection of events. In 2005, Austin adopted this idea that originated in Boston and which has been taken up by many other cities, and the debut was a big success. The signature event was a parade downtown with all sorts of participants, from a Segway ballet to a thirty-foot tall papier-mâché Stevie Ray Vaughan to a marching theremin player. The parade wrapped up with hundreds of people carrying loaves of bread. Event organizers had delivered 2,006 loaves to the doors of random people during the night and asked them to bring their bread and march. Along with all sorts of music and dance events scattered around downtown, there were fake snow, people in business suits repelling off buildings, and a failed attempt to do the world's longest artwork by having a chalk drawing that stretched across Town Lake on the South 1st Street Bridge. But why is it called First Night? Why not Last Night? Too apocalyptic?

An ecumenical Christmas decoration at the Cosmic Café.

The Christmas display at the GSDM building on West 6th Street is actually made up of living armadillos and snowmen.

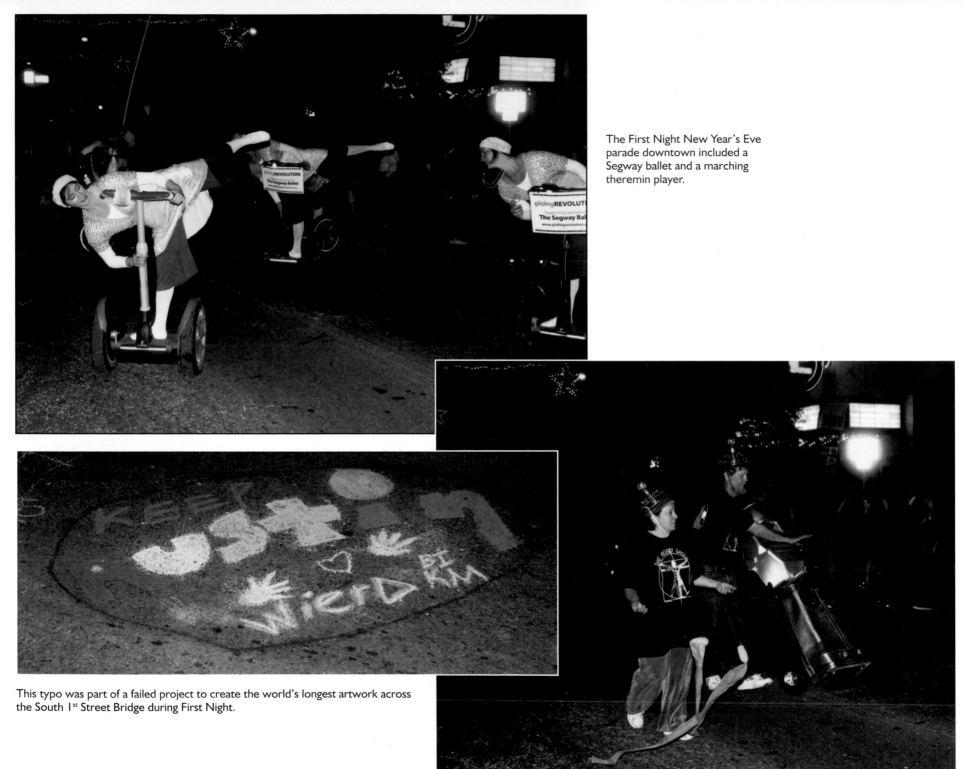

The First Night New Year's Eve parade downtown included a Segway ballet and a marching theremin player.

This typo was part of a failed project to create the world's longest artwork across the South 1st Street Bridge during First Night.

Chapter 5.
Weird Radio

Radio and the web are the mass media that let the little guy have a shot. The web is such a shape shifter, to try to document all the weird Austin sites would lead to future frustration. (www.keepaustinweird.com/links.html has a collection.) But radio is relatively stable and there are several good—and many bad—radio stations in Austin.

KOOP, 91.7 – The station that inspired the phrase that launched a thousand shirts. It was while phoning in a pledge to this station that the author of this book said he was giving because the station, specifically *The Lounge Show*, "helps keep Austin weird."

The station is all-volunteer (well, there's one employee), which leads to highly idiosyncratic programming. *Graveside Service* plays tunes on the death anniversary of musicians. *Really Motional Music* "features artists with known mental health and/or substance abuse issues." On Sunday mornings the *Czech Melody Hour* is followed by a show of reggae oldies called *Jamaican Gold*. There are lots more alternative musical, political, and social programming. See the complete schedule and listen online at www.koop.org.

Jay Robillard, host of *The Lounge Show* (Saturdays, 10:00 AM – noon), is an encyclopedia of easy-listeningiana. He received 10,000 LPs when his father closed a radio station he owned in Louisiana. This formed the core of Jay's massive collection of mainstream lounge (Perry Como, Dean Martin) and loony crooners (Lee Marvin singing "I Was Born Under a Wandering Star," Bridget Bardot's "Soixante Neuf"). His show regularly wins a "Best of Austin" award in the *Austin Chronicle*'s reader's poll.

Jay is one of those examples of the bedrock weirdness of Austin. His show is very weird and very popular, but Jay is a down-to-earth, genial guy who leads an outwardly normal life, overseeing installations of outdoor lighting as a day job. (Can outdoor lighting be a *day* job?) He and his lovely wife, Melinda, also run a DJ business, All Retro Music, from which you can add a touch of funk to your next party.

KOOP shares its frequency, 91.7, with **KVRX**, a station that takes over at 7:00 PM on weekdays and at 10:00 PM on weekends and goes overnight until 9:00 AM. (Actually they're on twenty-four hours; vampire-like, during the day it's only on the Internet.) The station plays edgy music and pleasantly uncomfortable programming and the occasional high school football game, hosted by the students at the University of Texas. See the huge schedule and listen online at www.kvrx.org.

Jay Robillard's *The Lounge Show* on KOOP led to the invention of Keep Austin Weird.

Radio Free Austin is loony (or is it the truth?) politics at its best. This is a low-power station so it isn't licensed by those nazi communists at the FCC, thus there are different frequencies in different parts of town (100.1 works in central Austin as of this writing). The star is nationally renowned but Austin's own Alex Jones (www.infowars.com). His anti-Bush rants are music to Austin's left-wing, even if he is ultimately against them too. Jones is on from 11:00 AM – 2:00 PM, repeated at 10:00 PM. Some of the other shows are dreary droners pushing Jesus' plan to control the weather, but sometimes nothing beats a good conspiracy theorist. www.radiofreeaustin.org

KUT, 90.5, the local NPR station, is generally above average and has a loyal following. It promotes the local music scene with lots of live performances and gets very high Arbitron ratings, higher than the great majority of commercial stations. It easily raises donations of over a million dollars a year, equal to NPR stations in Dallas and Houston, towns that have two to three times more population.

Recommended local shows: *Eklektikos*, Monday – Friday, 9:00 AM – 12:00 PM. DJ John Aielli has hosted this adventurous show since the early 1970s. He does frequent eccentric themes, tying together classical, pop, folk, and bizarre tunes. Two examples: an hour built on the writer Katherine Anne Porter and another on cherry pie, inspired by his fondness for the TV show *Twin Peaks*.

Other faves: *The Phil Music Show*, Thursday, 8:00 – 11:00 PM. *Left of the Dial*, Friday, 8:00 – 11:00 PM. You can listen online at www.kut.org.

> In the spring 2005 semester, the Communications department at the University of Texas actually offered a course called Keep Austin Weird Radio. Students built radios out of sequin-covered taco shells and broadcast Don Knotts impersonators covering women's wrestling.

KGSR, 107.1 – This station isn't exactly weird, but deserves a kudo (those would be good call letters) for playing lots of local music, both recorded and live. They also play a more eclectic blend than other commercial stations. Lyle Lovett might be followed by Bob Marley then Fountains of Wayne. They also support many good causes. You can listen online at www.kgsr.com.

KAOS, at 92.7 and 95.9 and online at www.kaos959.com, is anarchistic, hardcore, whatever music. With shows such as *How To Deal With Italian Sauce starring Detergent* and *Saturday Night Drunk Club*, you get the idea.

Chapter 6
Weird Outdoor Art and Art Cars

Whether they come from innocents with inner visions or knowing artsy types or even from businesses, Austin has a nice selection of various kinds of outdoor art. Unlike some of the weirder aspects of our city, these are not so concentrated in certain areas; there is outdoor art scattered all around, as if some plant had spread its odd seeds to the four winds. (Also see the chapter Weird Places.)

The cement gorilla on West Lynn dresses up for special occasions, as you'll see elsewhere in this book. Here he welcomes the arrival of summer.

One of the best examples of a decorated yard is Ira Poole's corner lot at 2400 E. Martin Luther King. His combination of a Statue of Liberty, a concrete map of the U.S., an Egyptian sphinx, topiary shrubs, and painted tree trunks, makes for a lovely spot. If he should be out in his yard, say hello. He's a very amiable man.

This yard in east Austin is completely lined with plastic bottles filled with water. This practice is seen occasionally in other yards and evidently is meant to keep either dogs or evil spirits out. In any case, it's a lovely site when coupled with some nicely shaped shrubs, as here.

This extravagant collection of statuary is in the 1900 block of Paramount in the 78704 part of South Austin.

A stunning yard done by Beth Thom at the corner of West 29th and Glenview. She originally did it a few years earlier and revived it in 2005. The house that goes with it has all sorts of interesting features too.

This Venus on the half-shell belongs to the author and was hand painted by artist David Elliott. The dog is Tillie.

A house in Clarksville, by MoPac, that belongs to Aralyn Hughes, is not subtle in making its point.

Mangia is a local pizza chain that features a Godzilla-like mascot on its stores and delivery vehicles. In 2005, this particular monster on Guadalupe Street was cruelly pushed off the roof and smashed. Plastic surgeons from Japan were flown in and repaired him, costing over $33 million and paid for by the estate of Raymond Burr.

A group called Capital Area Statues (www.capitalareastatues.com), composed of various local heroes such as singer Marcia Ball, writers Stephen Harrigan, Bill Wittliff, and Lawrence Wright, has been responsible for a couple of traditional sculptures of nontraditional subjects. Philosophers' Rock, erected in 1994, is near Barton Springs Pool, the very popular natural spring swimming hole that has water with a year round temperature of -40 degrees and is over thirty miles long. Its up-and-down pollution levels are the stuff of great controversy. The philosophers depicted are J. Frank Dobie, Roy Bedichek, and Walter Prescott Webb, natural and unnatural historians at the University of Texas in the 1950s. They frequently met at the pool to bump their gums about matters philosophical. They are widely regarded as the city's sex symbols.

The Philosophers' Rock honors intellectual sunbathers.

The Philosophers' Rock is part of Barton Springs Pool, the environmental canary in the Austin coalmine.

The other statue this group has sponsored is of Angelina Eberly, the woman who prevented Houston from stealing the state archives in that benighted city's attempt to move the capital there (see Weird Politics chapter for more). She alerted the *gendarmes* of the robbery by firing a cannon on Congress Avenue, the main downtown street, where the statue is located.

Angelina Eberly, the heroine of the Archive War.

Famous professional golfer Stevie Ray Vaughan was dipped in bronze and set up by Town Lake in 1994.

There are a fair number of art cars in town, although it's sad to say it pales next to Houston, which has an impressively bizarre number of and devotion to them (www.orangeshow.org/artcar.html).

Every fall there's a parade down Congress Avenue, culminating at the hip South Congress area, where geeks can gawk at them up close. (See the Weird Events chapter for more.)

With traffic so congested, a concerted movement for more art cars is needed to give idling motorists something to look at. I appeal to the weirdoes of Austin to accept the challenge and take away Houston's title of Art Car Capital (plus it would help get back at those bastards for trying to steal the republic's archives back in 1842 and make their swamp city the capital).

If unusual but more genteel ways to travel appeal to you, there's a Segway tour of downtown Austin (www.segcity.com) and a riverboat tour of Town Lake (www.lonestarriverboat.com), which is a good way to watch the bats emerge at sunset.

The pig car belongs to Aralyn Hughes, who has a pet pig who often drives around town on his own.

This truck belongs to the author.
It was painted by C. Thresher
and David Elliott.

A wonderful car that
lives in south Austin.

Easily the best business sign in town. So honest. This is at Walker Tire Company on Airport Blvd.

The "Hi, How Are You" mural on West 21st Street, near the U.T. campus, has a story that suits Austin well. Done by oddball indie musician, Daniel Johnston in 1993 on the side of a local record store, it was going to be destroyed when the space was converted to a franchise restaurant in 2004. Fans rallied, national press converged, and the mural was saved at a cost to the new owner of $50,000. The restaurant has folded but the frog lives on.

A couple of commercial artists who create large-scale projects that aim for the odd side are Blue Genie Art Industries (www.bluegenieart.com), who do murals, Styrofoam sculptures, art cars, and all sorts of other things; and Bob "Daddy-o" Wade (bobwade.com), who does definitely strange works in a variety of media.

This is the corporate vehicle for Blue Genie Art.

A mural on West 5th Street done by Rory Skagen, who is part of Blue Genie Art.

These two works adorn the yard of Faith Schexnayder in south Austin on West Gibson Street. She is an artist who works in carved foam, such as this chicken, and ceramics, such as this quilt, and other media. See more of her work at www.flatforkstudio.com.

Chapter 7
Weird Politics

ustin was born of politics and it has led to some strange "bedpersons." In 1839 the tiny settlement of Waterloo was designated to become the capital of the new Republic of Texas and was named Austin to honor Stephen F. Austin, early colonist and ungrateful rebel against the Mexicans who had given him lots of land. (In gratitude for getting rid of the name Waterloo, which leaves such a bitter taste in the mouths of the French, one of the first buildings constructed in Austin was the French Legation, still a boring tourist spot. France was the only country other than the U.S. to officially recognize Texas as an independent republic.)

Creeps from the town of Houston wanted *it* to be the capital and tried to steal the republic's archives in 1842. As they carted them out of town in the middle of the night, Angelina Eberly, a bawdy-house mistress, spied them and fired a cannon that was lying around downtown. An alerted vigilante squad pursued the Houstonians and recaptured the archives. As further punishment, they put a curse on the out-of-towners that their baseball team would never win the World Series.

The most famous politician to be associated with Austin—although he really was from Stonewall—was Lyndon Johnson. Perhaps his greatest claim to fame was owning the only TV station in town, KTBC, until the 1970s. KTBC actually had a show in the 1950s called "Captain Superior" where a man read the comics from the newspaper out loud and which yours truly faithfully watched. Johnson's influence is still seen today in the really hideous LBJ Library on the University of Texas campus. The most notable exhibits within are the objects ordinary citizens gave the president and the robot version of LBJ that tells jokes.

Austin is famous for being a liberal oasis in thoroughly conservative Texas and is referred to both scoffingly and proudly as "The Peoples Republic of Austin." While every statewide political office was (and still is) held by a Republican in 2000, and the state gave fake native son George W. Bush (he was born in Connecticut) fifty-nine percent in the presidential election, there were several precincts in Austin where Bush came in *third*, behind Gore and Nader. In the 2005 election on a state constitutional amendment outlawing same-sex marriage, Travis County, wherein Austin lies, was the only one in the entire state to vote against it, and did so by a three-to-two margin. Our district attorney, Ronnie Earle, indicted slimy congressman Tom DeLay on corruption charges, helping lead to his resignation, and nationally known liberal commentator Molly Ivins is a longtime resident.

Austin was the first and still the only city in Texas to elect an openly gay representative to the state legislature. The sheriff of Travis County in the late 1990s was a lesbian. Think about that: in Texas, a sheriff who was not just a female but also a lesbian.

The avant-garde architecture of the LBJ Library is a complex metaphor for governmental operations.

The gifts to LBJ from a confused nation are a nifty part of the LBJ Library.

70

The current mayor has the perfect politician name: Will Wynn. Before being mayor, he was a city councilperson and chaired an economic development committee. One of the main portions of their white paper advocated "Keep Austin Weird" as a way to draw hip, bright young things with their high-paying high-tech and creative jobs.

All politics is loco, and Austin's had some real doozies.

The city government formally acknowledges the benefits of weirdness.

The mayor of Austin, Will Wynn, knows a good slogan when he hears one.

Leslie Cochran – The most famous of Austin's current eccentrics, this homeless cross-dresser has run for mayor or city council three times, receiving up to eight percent of the vote. He ran on a platform of platform shoes.

Jennifer Gale – A transsexual homeless perennial candidate for mayor, city council, U.S. Congress, and the Austin school board. She got forty percent of the vote in the latter race in 2004 and forced a runoff. In 2006 she got over six percent in her run for mayor.

Frequent political candidate Leslie Cochran is a man and woman of the people.

Richard Goodman – A popular TV news anchor turned city councilperson. His promising career was cut short in 1982 when he was arrested for firing nineteen shots at his garden hose, insisting, due to cocaine-induced hallucinations, there were snakes attacking him.

John Johnson – A Mafia hitman turned stoolie was living in Austin under the witness protection program and operating a hot dog stand on 6th Street. What better qualifications for a mayoral candidate? Not only did he blow his cover, but he also got only .24 percent of the vote in 1997.

Paul Spragens – Absurdist city council candidate in 1975. Among his many sterling ideas were legalizing dueling and creating dueling greens in the parks, turning the police fleet into a free taxi service, and a promise to have a TV always on in his office for constituents to watch soaps and game shows. His greatest idea was to require all candidates to file a formal full disclosure of their power fantasies. Spragens got 1,380 votes.

Crazy Carl Hickerson – Using the old Soviet acronym CCCP, Crazy Carl for Council Person, he ran multiple times, from 1977 to 1996. Widely recognized on the street as a flower peddler with an uncanny knack for spinning a mum on one finger, he normally got about one percent of the vote. In his 1977 run, famous atheist Madalyn Murray O'Hair was running for a different seat on the council. In a voter's forum she said she and Carl were the "only serious candidates." Since retiring from politics, Carl has dedicated his time to growing female-sized breasts through the use of a suction device.

??? and ??? – This pair ran sometime in the 1980s for council on the platform of having no platform. They advocated installing a citywide in-home electronic network where everyone would vote on every issue, and they dutifully showed up at all the political forums and would answer each question by saying, "My personal opinion isn't important, because with the network you could…." Sadly, they didn't win. I cannot find any history on this pair, names, year, anything. Maybe I dreamed them.

Austin's mayoral race is guaranteed to bring out some weirdoes. *Drawing by C. Thresher.*

Kinky Friedman – This part-time Austinite (he also lives in Medina, Texas) is, as of this writing, pursuing the governorship as an independent. A musician (Kinky Friedman and the Texas Jewboys) and best-selling novelist, Kinky is running on a pleasantly inconsistent set of issues, ranging from greatly increasing teacher salaries to putting the Ten Commandants everywhere to outlawing the declawing of cats. One of his slogans is "How Hard Could It Be?" Creepy politico hack State Comptroller Carol Strayhorn was also running as an independent candidate and also had to gather thousands of signatures to get on the ballot, and Friedman got more verified signatures. But according to a state assistant attorney general, "the Strayhorn campaign dismisses Friedman as the 'Keep Austin Weird' crowd." Kinky, however, wrote the following in *Texas Monthly*: "The rest of Texas vilifies Austin as a breeding ground for long-haired hell-raisers. To me, it's an open-minded, open-hearted, magical little town—and always will be."

Jay Adkins and Skip Slyfield – This pair won the presidency and vice presidency of the University of Texas student government running on the Arts and Sausages ticket in 1977, using the slogan "Money Talks." Student government was disbanded at the end of their administration.

Kinky Friedman is a man of the weird people.

This trailer hauls around Kinky's daily allotment of cigars.

Four for Texas – Your humble author was one of a quartet who ran for U.T. student government president in 1973 on a joint ticket. That is Rick Day, David Elder, John White, and yours truly all ran for the same office at the same time and had joint campaign literature. Our various platforms included tonsillectomies on demand; a vow that Walter Cronkite would mention them on the news; having a request line for the university tower chimes; and one man, one channel. A tiresome number of people, including supporters, pointed out that we would do better if we just ran one person instead of four.

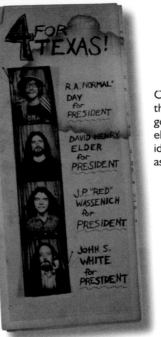

Campaign literature from the 4 for Texas student government presidency election in 1973 at U.T. Four idiots ran for the same office as a team.

For over four months in 1988 and 1989 a group of homeless people floated on three homemade rafts in the middle of Austin on Town Lake threatening to kill their hostage goose, Homer, to protest the lack of affordable housing and services for the downtrodden. They had cleverly bought a fishing permit and constantly kept a pole in the water, thus legally fending off the city's attempts to get rid of the daily reminder of the considerable number of homeless in town. A banner saying "Homer says help the homeless" festooned the flotilla, and the story got legs, drawing reporters from around the country and even Australia. Homer even attended the 1988 Democratic National Convention to honk on behalf of the homeless. Finally, the city passed a law targeting the group and they were removed. "Homeless and boatless" they proclaimed. But happily their protest was wildly successful and Austin solved the problems and total social equity was achieved.

Homer was taken in by a local couple as a pet and, in 2006, they had to give him up so they could travel in their retirement. A party to memorialize the raft adventure and to find now eighteen-year-old Homer a new home was held at Town Lake. Twenty-five people applied to become Mother Goose.

Neighborhood favorite Nik the Goat was granted a pardon by the mayor so he could remain a city dweller.

In other animal news, Mayor Will Wynn in 2005 granted a "pardon" to Nik the Goat, who lives in a front yard on Mary Street, just west of South Congress. Although a friendly neighborhood figure, he was in violation of some esoteric livestock code and the city was going to exile him. Public outcry led to his exemption. Drop by and give him a scratch (the goat or the mayor).

The Austin City Council opens with a prayer from a local pastor. Here's a portion of the invocation from Vance Russell:

I pray that a spirit of repentance come upon your people for breaking their relationship with you. I ask that you forgive Austin for pursuing false religions. Forgive us for creating idols in place of worshiping you. Lord, you are jealous over Austin. This city is not weird.

The new Austin City Hall, which opened in 2006, brought out diametrically opposed opinions on its modern architecture, but everyone agrees that the "Pinocchio nose" feature is wonderful. With each lie told by the city council, the nose grows one inch. This photo was taken less than six months after its inception.

Chapter 8
Weird Shopping

Shopping is not the first thing that pops into my mind when I think of weirdness, and in fact the whole "shopping as sport" mindset is sort of creepy. However both because Austin is blessed with an abundance of odd shops and to pander to the sort of people I imagine would buy this stupid book, here goes.

As discussed in the opening chapter, the phrase Keep Austin Weird is thought of by many if not most as a marketing slogan to promote local businesses, which was not the intent when it was invented. But in the marketplace of ideas, that's what happened and that's OK.

There's no way I can list all the appropriate businesses, so the following present a decent sample of ones where the needle gets into the red area on the "weirdometer." By their very nature, these seem to come and go pretty often (but that's true for all small businesses). For a more complete listing of local business, weird and otherwise, visit the Austin Independent Business Alliance website: www.ibuyaustin.com.

Most of the ones listed show up in geographical pockets, so they are discussed by area rather than type of business, with a miscellaneous category for the strays.

South 1st Street

South 1st has the best concentration of truly weird businesses, and that isn't widely acknowledged. From about a mile south of the river to Oltorf there are dozens of small, strange shops, with a leavening of Mexican restaurants and mechanics to keep it real. This brings up the point that true weirdness seems to almost require a lack of notoriety to thrive—sort of the mushroom in the coalmine. Once something weird gets general acceptance, the bloom is off the rose and the blandness virus moves in, to use a Slurpee of metaphors. The South Congress (SoCo) area that is famous as an alternative commercial area is exhibit A. Although it still has some cool stuff and is covered herein, it is rapidly losing its alt feel and becoming a yuppie expensive ghetto. So why don't I shut up and not publicize the good stuff so it will stay weird? Hmmm. My guess is vanity. And this process has really started: www.sofi.com is promoting many of the businesses along South 1st.

Todd Sanders, the friendly owner of **Roadhouse Relics**, has created a fantastic collection of signs, neon, and objects that you would swear are from forty or fifty years ago. He refers to it as "modern vintage." His website has a nice selection of these and describes his techniques. When I commented that South 1st had much weirder stores than South Congress, Todd said, "SoCo stands for So Conventional." 1720 South 1st Street. www.road houserelics.com

Todd Sanders of Roadhouse Relics amidst his "modern vintage" creations.

If any picture captures weird Austin, this is it.

On South 1st Street is the "corporate headquarters" for the **Soup Peddler**. Dave Ansel started delivering his hand-made soup to subscribers' homes on his bicycle. It became so successful he's had to add a fleet of riders and some vans even. His customers are fanatics, calling themselves Soupies. They rave about the gourmet soups and even have a blog and online discussion board. The Soup Peddler has recently gotten national press and has expanded into entrees and desserts, causing chatter among devotees about whether success is unfunkifying a once quirky business. The story of Austin in a nutshell. 501 West Mary (corner of South 1st Street). www.souppeddler.com

(Also see in the Weird Food and Drink chapter Bouldin Creek Café.)

Secret Oktober is an example of the many small shops on South 1st. It refers to itself as a source of "Gothic punk alternative clothing." 1905 South 1st Street. www.secret-oktober.com

The shops at 2209 South 1st are alternative, local ones that haven't gotten too successful to turn into South Congress yet. They're not too crowded, you can park, and the folks are friendly.

South Lamar

There are many nontraditional shopping opportunities in the three miles from south of the river on Lamar. One must watch for the occasional Starbucks, but generally it's pretty high on the oddness scale, and there are still enough upholstery stores and porn shops to tamp down the glitz. Too bad it's so difficult to cross the street.

The shopping center in the 1000 block of South Lamar has a nifty variety of off-kilter stores, from a Salvation Army to a new age book store to multiple vintage shops. One of the branches of the highly recommended Alamo Draft Houses is here too.

Floribunda is a cool small nursery that makes the phrase "yard art" literal by fashioning furniture out of turf grass. There's usually some other art strewn around. A friendly local place. 2041 South Lamar. www.floribunaworks.com

Planet K, a shop with smoking accessories and other vaguely society-threatening items, has one of its four Austin locations at 1516 South Lamar. There's also a coffee stand called the Grateful Shed.

This Planet K also houses the **South Austin Museum of Popular Culture**, which has works by Austin artists, including many classic music posters by studs such as Jim Franklin. Outside there's a wall of memorials to dead Texas musicians from Tex Ritter to Biscuit Turner. www.samopc.org

(Also see in the Weird Food and Drink chapter Maria's Taco Xpress and the Broken Spoke.)

This lovely planter is around back at Planet K on South Lamar.

Dead Texas musicians are memorialized outside the South Austin Museum of Popular Culture.

South Congress

The main street of Austin, from south of Riverside Drive to Oltorf, was, starting in the early 1990s, an innovative haven for weird shopping but has become largely a chic-dom of pricey touristy businesses—sort of a canary in a gilded coalmine. Happily most businesses are still locally owned, and there are still a good number of weirder ones, a selection of which is listed here. In addition to shopping, SoCo is also a major area to hang out, so some of those spots are listed here too. First Thursday is a monthly event when the shops stay open late and bands play and the hordes descend (www.first thursday.info).

Looking for that hat rack made from a girdle or Japanese medical posters from the 1930s? **Uncommon Objects** is a stellar collection of vendors under one roof. Invariably you will find something nutso that you'll drool over. A constantly changing inventory at this well-named store and usually reasonable prices make it the star of SoCo. 1512 South Congress. www. uncommonobjects. com

The outside décor alone justifies **Lucy in Disguise with Diamonds/Electric Ladyland**. Inside there is a huge inventory of vintage and hip clothes and accessories plus an extensive costume rental collection. Try getting near this place around Halloween. 1506 South Congress. www.lucyindisguise.com

The **Austin Motel** is one of the pioneers that helped transform SoCo from trashy to flashy. Family-owned since 1938, this vintage motel on the old highway to San Antonio had, like most of the surrounding area, grown seedy. But in the 1980s, current owner, Dottye Dean, started renovating it back to its glory days and a trend took root. A good interior Mexican restaurant, El Sol y La Luna, is also on the grounds. 1220 South Congress. www.austinmotel.com

Jo's Hot Coffee and Good Food is an unpretentious but hip hangout that's excellent for watching the bohemians. It only has outdoor seating, so bring your dog. On the First Thursday monthly extravaganzas (see above), Jo's offers valet bicycle parking. They also host occasional outdoor movies and live bands. 1300 South Congress. www.joscoffee.com

Jo's has hipsters and their dogs and **PDAs**. *Drawing by C. Thresher.*

The **Continental Club** has been going since 1957. What was originally a classy nightspot in the 1950s devolved into a strip club in the '60s and in the '70s went even lower to its current incarnation, happily becoming a roots rock dive. One of the iconic live music venues in Austin that's still going. 1315 South Congress. www.continentalclub.com/Austin.html

The **Great Outdoors Nursery** is a ways south of the hip SoCo area, which ain't a bad thing, and worth a visit. In addition to a nice plant selection, they go beyond garden gnomes with their yard art and planters. There's even a latte-serving café here. 2730 South Congress. www.gonursery.com

The Great Outdoors Nursery can help weirdify your yard.

Tesoros Trading Company is actually on North Congress, in the heart of downtown. Stores selling imports from around the world are commonplace throughout the country these days, but Tesoros walks that extra mile. In addition to the usual colorful woven goods and papier-mâché satans, you find wrestling masks, Mexican movie posters, communist Chinese propaganda, odd medical posters from India, et cetera. Now the bad news: This block is scheduled to be turned into a Brobdingnagian hotel complex that will displace Tesoros and its cool next door neighbor, **Las Manitas Avenue Café**, which is famed for its eclectic clientele and excellent affordable Tex-Mex fare. Who needs such things? Wouldn't you prefer a $180-a-night hotel room? 209 Congress. www.tesoros.com

The appealing combo of Las Manitas and Tesoros is in limbo with the demolition ball of Damocles hanging over its head.

Tesoros is crammed with the loot of the world.

North Loop Street/53rd Street

The 100 block of East North Loop and nearby East 53rd Street have a cluster of cool businesses. To say the least, there's a notable difference in feel from South Congress. This is much more blue-collar funky and thank goodness.

Room Service is an excellent store packed with vintage clothes, retro tschotkes, furniture, and jewelry at good prices. They've been going since 1981. A second branch opened in the cool South Lamar area in 2006. 107 East North Loop and 1701 South Lamar. www.roomservicevintage.com

Room Service has a wonderful mix of furniture, art, clothes.

Velvet and paint-by-number works and gaudy lamps make a house a home.

Room Service also sells fine reading matter.

Some other stores in this neck of the woods that cater to the retro and weirdo crowd are **Austin Modern Vintage** (207 East 53rd), **Hogwild Texas** (vintage clothes, furniture, toys) (100 East North Loop), **Sound on Sound** (new and used vinyl and CDs) (106 East North Loop), and **MonkeyWrench Books** (a collectively owned radical bookstore) (110 East North Loop).

A selection of Unemployed Democrats bumper stickers, along with piñatas of ex-Congressman Tom DeLay and Governor Rick Perry.

Miscellaneous Locations

Unemployed Democrats is a business that signals Austin's difference, especially from the rest of very red Texas. Founded in 2000 as a reaction to George W. Bush's fake election victory, this business—largely web-based—promulgates bumper stickers, shirts, buttons, piñatas, and such, cleverly attacking the Grand Old Party. We took some visitors from China to this store and they were very impressed. "You would not see a store devoted to attacking our president in China." So weirdoes are patriotic too. 909 W. Mary Street (part of Cafe Caffeine).
www.unemployed democrats.com

Bob Henson, owner of Unemployed Democrats, holds his signature item.

Moxie and the Compound features only clothes, accessories, and art, mainly of the somewhat wacky variety, made by Austinites. Kayci Wheatley is the genial owner and is dedicated to not ripping off the designers, giving them a bigger cut than do other shops. Located in the heart of the up-and-coming area just off South 5th Street at 909 West Mary, Suite B. www.moxieandthecompound.com

Kayci Wheatley of Moxie and the Compound sells locally designed odder fashions.

BookPeople, as discussed in the opening chapter, is an excellent bookstore that is a leader in the movement to promote Austin businesses over national chains. In addition to having a strong book collection, they host many author visits, a mix of local and world-famous. They distribute free Keep Austin Weird bumper stickers and sell a variety of KAW merchandise. An excellent collection of strange toys and odd candy lines the stairs. Lamar at 6th Street. www.bookpeople.com

If mere books aren't enough for you, BookPeople stocks lots of Keep Austin Weird knickknacks.

Every self-respecting liberal town needs a feminist bookstore, and Austin's BookWoman (1918 West 12th, ebookwoman.booksense.com) has been going since the 1970s. They also stock Keep Austin (fill in the blank) products.

Austin is the Live Music Capital of the World but it has got to have a solid source of recorded music to go along with that. **Waterloo Records** fills that role with ease. A strong collection of popular music of all sorts and a friendly staff who know scary amounts about it plus lots of free in-store performances have made Waterloo one of the important parts of the music scene. Once when considering a gift to send to a friend in England, I asked a clerk about whether various Austin artists' albums had been distributed over there. Without hesitating he knew the answers and proceeded on to explain whether they had also toured there. Waterloo coupled with nearby BookPeople to promote Keep Austin Weird in the fight to support local businesses. 600 North Lamar. www.waterloorecords.com

Groovy Lube, an oil change business on Guadalupe Street, is one of those touches that shows how Austin is a wee bit different. It's not real likely that in any other city in Texas would such a place use that name and have a peace symbol as its logo.

The **Whip-In** makes the usual nightmare of a convenience store into a pleasure. The very friendly owner, Dipak Topiwala ("your beer-wala"), runs a classy but goofy store that features a massive collection of beer and wine, plus the grocery section goes beyond Slim Jims into gourmet cheeses and sandwiches. Rather than Skoal, you can get a fine cigar. With a bow to his heritage, there are also various Indian fabrics and sculptures for sale. A crowning touch is the seating area with a piano ready for the random artiste. Whip-In sponsors a charity concert at the Continental Club on the first Sunday of the month. They also sell Keep Austin Weird bumper stickers. 1950 South I-35 (on the west access road). www.whipin.com

Dipak Topiwala, owner and manager of Whip-In, enjoys an impromptu barrelhouse piano concert by a customer.

Oat Willie's has been around since the 1960s supplying paraphernalia and assorted oddities. Their clarion cry, "Onward Through the Fog," has been a bumper sticker on every Volkswagen that ever lived in Austin. Doug Brown, longtime owner, was somehow honored by the Texas State Senate in 2001. A source of Keep Austin Weird bumper stickers. 617 West 29th and 1931 East Oltorf

Snake Eyes Vinyl is a record and CD shop that regularly hosts "Make Austin Weirder Fests" with live hardcore bands at their store. 1211 East 7th Street. www.snakeeyesvinyl.com

Toy Joy, 2900 Guadalupe, offers a great collection of toys for all ages. Bizarre Asian gadgets, hip retro decorations, weird science projects, robots, et cetera. Their website (www.toyjoy.com) has visual tours of the inventory.

If you ever need to store your collection of fur-covered, scorpion-filled bowling balls, this business is the place to go.

For that last bit of shopping you'll ever do.

Atomic City has an intense collection of arty shoes, clothes, robots, rubber chickens, postcards, windup toys, et cetera, and has been doing it since the early 1980s. The owner with the good eye for weird merchandise is the Prince, a longtime Austin bohemian who has never been seen without a Hawaiian shirt. 1700 San Antonio Street

The Prince, owner of Atomic City.

Strange shoes are an Atomic City specialty.

Chapter 9
Weird Sports

The University of Texas football team's official mascot celebrates their national championship in 2006.

Roller Derby

Austin led the renaissance in girl roller derby, starting in 2001, and surely has the highest per capita participation in the world. Austin doesn't even have a minor league baseball team—the nearest is in the boring bedroom 'burb Round Rock—but we have *two* female roller derby leagues, with a total of nine teams.

The Texas Rollergirls (www.txrollergirls.com) skate at Playland Skate Center, 8822 McCann (near 183 & Burnet) on a flat track, and the Lone Star Rollergirls (www.txrd.com) roll on a banked track at various venues, including the Convention Center in downtown Austin. The latter league starred in a thirteen-part reality series on the Arts and Entertainment network in 2005. The two leagues don't even skate against one another, and there's word on the street of bad blood between them. With teams such as the Hotrod Honeys, Hell Marys, and Putas del Fuego, the events are, of course, occasions of drinking and live music and serious skating.

A Texas Rollergirls all-star team, in black, crushes the Tucson Saddletramps.

A representative selection of the cool roller derby audience.

The girls' image of being dangerous hard-hearts was belied when this author accidentally ordered only one advanced ticket instead of two and faced standing in a long line for the second one. The black-clad tattooed derby queen who was also staffing the will-call table shrugged and pulled out a free pass and handed it over.

The scary Texas Rollergirls display their softer side during a halftime tricycle race.

In addition to keeping Austin weird, the Texas Rollergirls keep it beautiful by cleaning up a block of East Cesar Chavez Street.

Women's Tackle Football

The Austin Outlaws play full-contact tackle professional football and are part of the National Women's Football League. They play at House Park field in central Austin. Check their website at www.austinoutlaws.com.

Synchronized Swimming

The H2Hos: A Renegade Feminist Synchronized Swim Team is a group of women who do what they describe as "postmodern Esther Williams performance art." Their website states "the H2Hos share a belief in the transformational power of women's creative collaboration," then goes on to say "and there is nothing much else to do during Texas summers but swim!" They perform sporadically. Their website is also sporadic. Follow the events listings in the *Austin Chronicle* to try and catch them.

Petanque

France was the only country besides the U.S. to recognize Texas as an independent nation back in the 1830s and they built a legation that is now a museum. The Alliance Française d'Austin holds petanque tournaments the second and fourth Sundays of each month there. For you hillbillies, petanque is a game in which drunks throw metal balls on the ground.

Bowling

Along with shoe fetishists, the demographics for weirdos and bowling are pretty high. There's just something about combining beer and throwing multicolored sixteen-pound balls around that releases endorphins.

Easily the best bowling alley in Austin is Dart Bowl. It has several display cases of fantastic bowling kitsch, it has gay bowling leagues, and the café has remarkably greasy delicious enchiladas. Get 'em with the homemade dinner rolls, but don't try holding a bowling ball until after you've washed your hands or you'll break some toes. 5700 Grover.

The alley in the basement of the University of Texas Student Union offers glow-in-the-dark bowling Thursday through Sunday.

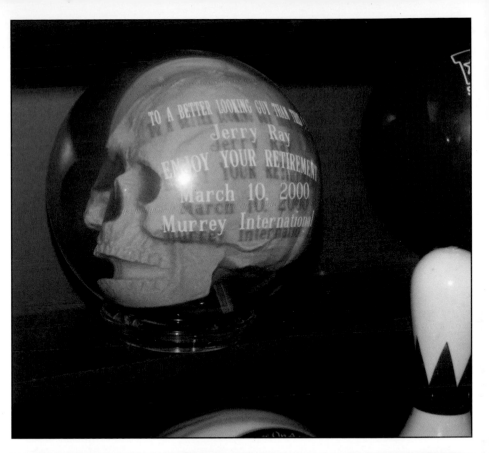

Dart Bowl has a large museum of bowling kitsch.

Miniature Golf

Perhaps the most sophisticated of all weirdo sports, miniature golf has a long history of appreciating the combination of art and athletics. Fortunately, Austin has a dilly of a course with Peter Pan Mini-Golf. This retro gem opened in 1948 and has never looked forward, thankfully. Most of the statues and assorted obstacles are original. The two eighteen-hole courses are filled with kiddie birthday parties, teens on first dates, and wizened beatniks. 1207 Barton Springs Road.

Right across the street is the nine-hole Butler Pitch and Putt, which has it's goofy side too. At the right time of year there will be banana and pear trees laden with fruit and parrots squawking in the trees. You'd think you were in heaven.

Most of the statuary at Peter Pan Mini-Golf is from the 1940s.

Peter Pan being stalked by a T-Rex.

Chapter 10
Weird Food and Drink

There are a goodly number of restaurants, bars, and coffee shops that cater to weirder tastes. As you'll see from the choices here, a favorite style is places that have maintained an old school feel against the tides of trendiness.

Restaurants

The **Texas Chili Parlor** has a timeless quality. It opened in 1976 and the interior and the staff rarely change (not meaning they don't change their underwear; they probably do). It's motto is "Don't you feel more like you do now than when you came?" There's a posted rule against talking to imaginary people. The location between the University of Texas and the state capitol leads to an eclectic crowd of punks and pols. Chili is a Blessed Sacrament in Texas, of course, and when the Chili Parlor introduced beans—deemed a Yankee perversion—as an option, there was outrage among some, and the daily paper covered the story for days. The Parlor stuck to its guns, and eventually the crisis and much gas passed.

Another high point came in 2003 in response to a news item that a restaurant in New York City was selling a $41 hamburger made from Kobe beef and other overpriced gourmet ingredients. The Chili Parlor developed their version of a $41 burger simply by multiplying the size of their normal $5 one, resulting in a twenty-four-pound, thirty-inch wide behemoth. 1409 Lavaca. www.cactushill.com/TCP/home.htm

Nau's Enfield Drug Store is a time capsule from the '50s. It opened in 1951, and about the only major change came a couple of years ago when they sold a $28 million dollar winning Lotto ticket to ex-Dallas Cowboy Hollywood Henderson and thus got a nice chunk of change. This prompted the radical move of switching from a mechanical cash register to an electronic one. The lunch counter has great and cheap cheeseburgers and real handmade milk shakes, ice cream sodas, and malts. The store stocks some products and gifts that seem like they're from about the time the store opened. It's a neat neighborhood scene, with many regulars who know each other and a friendly staff. Corner of West Lynn and West 12th Street

Nau's has the retro feel even down to the candy it stocks, featuring several you probably thought had disappeared, such as candy cigarettes, root beer barrels, Necco wafers, and chewing wax, plus newer treats such as a plastic nose that dispenses edible snot.

Dirty's (or its formal name, Martin's Kumbak) has been a great burger joint since 1926. It had a dirt floor until 1951, thus the name. The buns are so shiny with a tasty sheen of grease that you can see your own reflection. The onion rings are the best in town. Handmade malts and shakes add the extra calories we all need. The clientele is an entertaining mix of U.T. students, children, business people, politicians, and old timers attempting arterial suicide. Curb service is available, but we've never seen a person use it in the past thirty years. They've recently redecorated the interior and taken away a bit of the funk factor, but it's OK and the food remains greasalicious. 2808 Guadalupe. www.dirtymartins.com

The burgers and rings at Dirty's shine with greasy goodness.

Another throwback burger place—this one opened in 1961—is **Top Notch**. It has drive-in service or the lively sit-down area, which sports a nice collection of barbed wire mounted on Texas-shaped wood. Also one of the few non-franchise places that still serves fried chicken. 7525 Burnet Road

Fran's is a popular burger joint on South Congress that does it's part in the ongoing struggle.

Maria's Taco Xpress is a hip *tacqueria* in South Austin that is a Quetzalcoatl in the coalmine. In a neighborhood controversy, a chain drug store tore down the old version where Maria's has been, but a new, larger restaurant has gone in behind. Maria vows the funky quality will also move with it, but the old guard has seen this as another step toward blandification. Very crowded on weekends, Loca Maria, the owner, presides and a large sculpture of her graced the roof of the original site. In 2005 vandals broke her outstretched arms off, thus the bloody bandages in the photo. 2529 South Lamar. www.tacoxpress.com

Poor Loca Maria was disarmed by vandals in 2005.

El Arroyo Tex-Mex restaurant, the original location on West 5th Street, puts out a new message every day to greet drivers. The Ditch, as they refer to themselves, puts the fun ahead of the food, perhaps, and it can tend toward the party-hardy crowd, but they definitely don't take themselves too seriously. Nice outdoor eating area. 1624 West 5th Street. www.ditch.com

The El Arroyo catering bus.

The El Arroyo daily message on West 5th Street provokes thoughts in the commuters.

Here the fork in the road at Hyde Park Bar & Grill sports French fry candles to honor their twenty-third anniversary.

Sam's Bar-B-Que has the best in town. (There's a statement sure to lead to screaming arguments.) This superfunky joint in East Austin that has been going since the '80s is in a humble old house. The inside walls are plastered with posters for music events for next week and a decade ago. As with most 'que places, there's a suffusion of smoke on all surfaces. The brisket is recommended, but many opt for the mutton, not a common offering. 2000 E. 12th Street

Hyde Park Bar & Grill isn't particularly weird, although it's a convivial place with good food. But they do indulge in one oddity: the changing sculpture atop the "fork in the road." Other fork-toppers have been a Mr. Potato Head and a ten-foot-tall artichoke. 4206 Duval

The Broken Spoke is a honest-to-god honky-tonk. Begun in 1964 by James and Anneta White, who still own it, this restaurant and dance hall has hosted Bob Wills, Tex Ritter, Willie Nelson (well, duh), and hundreds of other country music acts. Folks go to dance and it's a pleasure to watch them two-step around the large floor. There's live music every night. The chicken fried steak is actually really good, a rarity. Inside, there's a "Tourist Trap Room" with photos and mementos from the club's history. Proof of the club's appeal and influence: Their website claims that a delegation of Soviet diplomats visited and said the Spoke was their favorite spot on their tour. Within two weeks of returning home, the Soviet Union fell. 3201 S. Lamar. www.brokenspokeaustintx.com

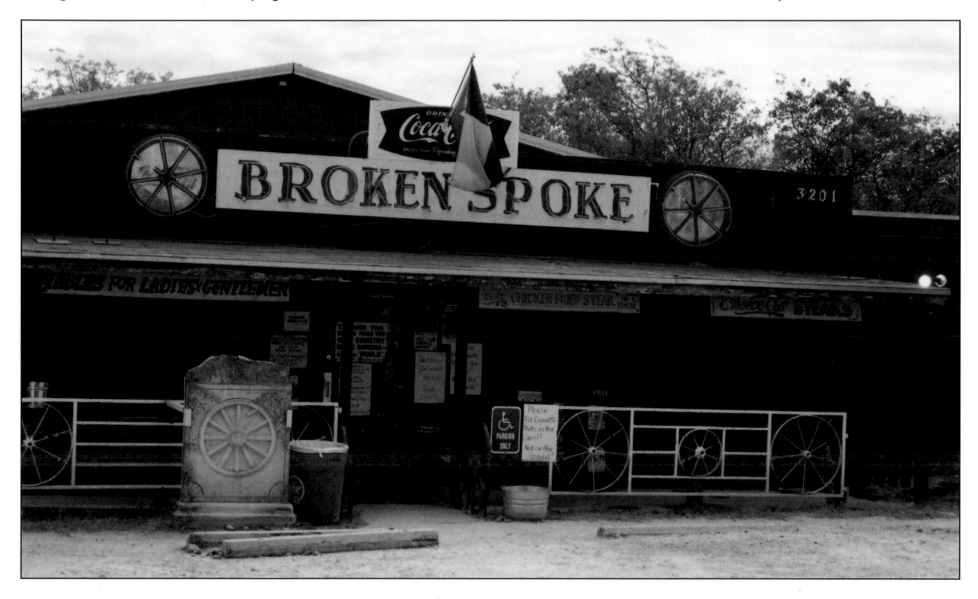

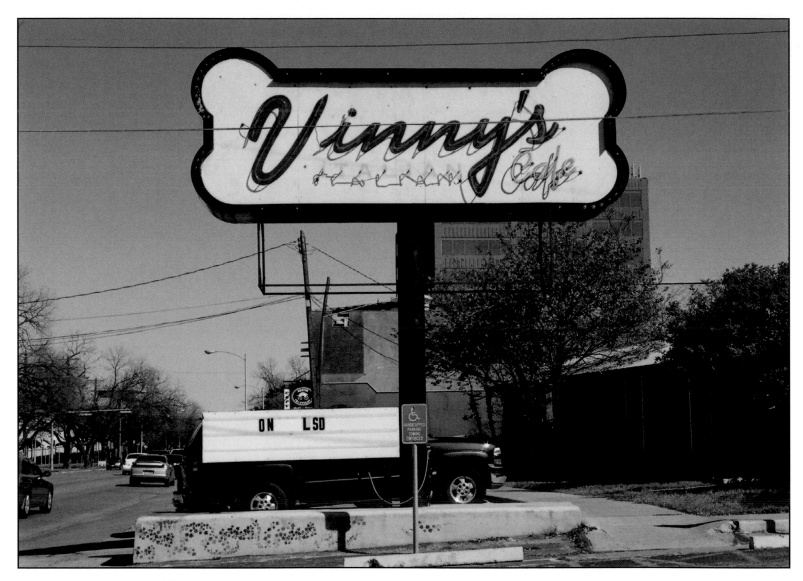

Normally **Vinny's** isn't regarded as a weird restaurant, but judging by this sign they do have a special secret ingredient.

Bars

For this listing of bars, I want to acknowledge the expert advice of Moira Muldoon, who has written the excellent biweekly column "A Girl Walks into a Bar" for the *XLent* section of the *Austin American-Statesman* since 2001. She knows lots of factoids and rumors about almost every high-class and low-rent bar in town. Two examples: Charlie's Attic (now where Barfly's is) on Airport Boulevard used to have one barstool that had a paint-shaker motor installed. When an attractive woman sat there, the bartender threw the switch. And a ghost haunts the bar at the upmarket Driskill Hotel, which is also where federal agents plotted the assault that killed Bonnie and Clyde.

A homemade cardboard shrine to *Iglesia de Musica* behind the bar, snapshots of deceased patrons on the wall, a picture of Karl Marx on the tip jar, a guy in a cowboy hat wearing an Artic Monkeys T-shirt, the click of dominoes being played by two generations of family give you a glimpse into the oddity of **Ginny's Little Longhorn Saloon**. This place is the perfect marriage of tradition and an unselfconscious weirdness. It's the sort of place you might be a bit nervous about going in. Dim lighting, peeling paint, the usual signs of a rough redneck bar disguise a really friendly, goofy joint. Owner Ginny Kalmbach and her daughter, Sharon, run the place with real charm. Live country and rockabilly music every night—really good, non-Nashville stuff—with no cover charge and cheap beer draw a swell mix.

The highlight of weirdness at Ginny's is on Sundays when "chickenshit bingo" happens. Between breaks by the band, Red (no relation to this author) is placed in a cage on a plywood sheet that's marked off with numbers and put on top of the pool table. The square he craps on picks the winner, who gets over $100 on a $2 ticket. Arguably the best bar in town to take a first date: If the person digs it, you got a winner. 5434 Burnet Road. www.ginnyslittlelonghorn.com

Red ponders his next move.

Another good throwback country joint is **Donn's Depot**, the only Austin bar listed in *Esquire*'s June 2006 collection of the best bars in the U.S. Composed of an old train depot and attached railroad cars—the ladies room is a caboose—Donn's opened in 1972. There is live music and dancing every night. About half the time the music is host Donn Adelman and the Station Masters. They have a swell smooth sound that gets them divorcees out on the floor. 1600 W. 5th Street. www.donnsdepot.com

A new and yet doomed entry in the alt country bar list is the **Mean-Eyed Cat**, named after a Johnny Cash song. Housed in a former chainsaw store just down the road from Donn's Depot, this beer joint has a younger, hipper crowd, but in a good way. A huge apartment complex is planned for the space the MEC occupies. Welcome to the new Austin. 1621 W. 5th Street.

The **Carousel Lounge** has a circus motif and a cool mixed-up feel and live music to match. Neighborhood old timers and young weirdoes mix in this north central Austin nightclub that opened in 1963 (supposedly named after Jack Ruby's Carousel Club in Dallas, which got famous quick that same year). The Austin club teeters back and forth from sort of seedy to knowingly hip. Lounge music one night, an indie pop band the next, followed by a roots rock group. 1110 E. 52nd Street.

The **Poodle Dog Lounge** can be found in the dictionary under "dive." A dark place with a mix of hipsters and rednecks drinking and playing shuffleboard (not the cruise ship kind) and shooting pool. A wall of photos of Marilyn Monroe and photo portraits of other dead movie beauties (who knows why?), a good jukebox, and live music make for a satisfying place to bend your elbow. 6507 Burnet.

Scholz Garten (frequently misnamed as Scholz's Garden) claims to be the oldest business in Texas. This German-style beer hall began in 1866, and it's close proximity to the state capitol and the University of Texas and the degenerate drunks those two places attract has kept it polkaing along. This is all exacerbated by its being a hangout for Democrats and football fans. How low can you go? Scholz is the only remaining German beer hall from what was once a flourishing feature of Austin. There were at least six huge establishments in the late nineteenth century. Scholz Garten, while large now, used to be much bigger and included fountains and a menagerie. A nice place to lounge on the patio and argue with people you agree with. 1607 San Jacinto. www.scholzgarten.net

Part of the space Scholz Garten occupies houses the Sängerrunde Singing Club, a German social organization formed in 1879, thus their claim to being the "oldest ethnic organization in Austin." Not only do they sing but they dance and bowl just as good as they want. Their old structure has a ballroom and a six-lane bowling alley.

The Dry Creek Cafe has been serving beer and sunsets since 1956. Only obstinance seems to hold up this ramshackle dive that used to be outside of town but that is now an amazing anachronism amid million-dollar lakeside mansions. Broken chairs fill the second-floor deck and broken-hearted songs fill the old-school jukebox. The bathrooms are shaky. Bring your empties back to the bar. 4812 Mount Bonnell Road

Coffee Shops

Austin, as should any self-respecting hipville, has plenty of cool independent coffee shops to counterbalance the Starbucks. A small sample of particularly good ones: **Spider House** (2908 Fruth. www.spider housecafe.com) near the university is a great spot in a rambling old house with a very nice outdoor area littered with odd art. In addition to the usual coffee and wifi, they offer films, live music, DJs, and other artsy events. **Bouldin Creek Café** (1501 South 1st Street. www.bouldincreek.com) is a pleasantly down home place in the current epicenter of true weirdo Austin with plenty of weirdo watching to go along with your caffeine and vegetarian food. There are lots of board games lying around to amuse you, plus outdoor seating. **Café Mundi** (1704 East 5th Street. cafemundi.com) in east Austin is sort of like a pub for wired slackers. Nice outdoor seating area. It's in an odd part of town on a sleepy industrial section of 5th Street that we guess will be one of the next big hip areas.

Spider House coffee shop, just north of U.T., is cooler than you are.

The Bouldin Creek Café is a vital part of the truly weird South 1st Street scene.

The "coffee shop dash" was a bike race and puzzle-solving event that hit eight of Austin's java joints.

There are lots of coffee shops filled with pale weirdoes writing manifestoes. *Drawing by C. Thresher.*

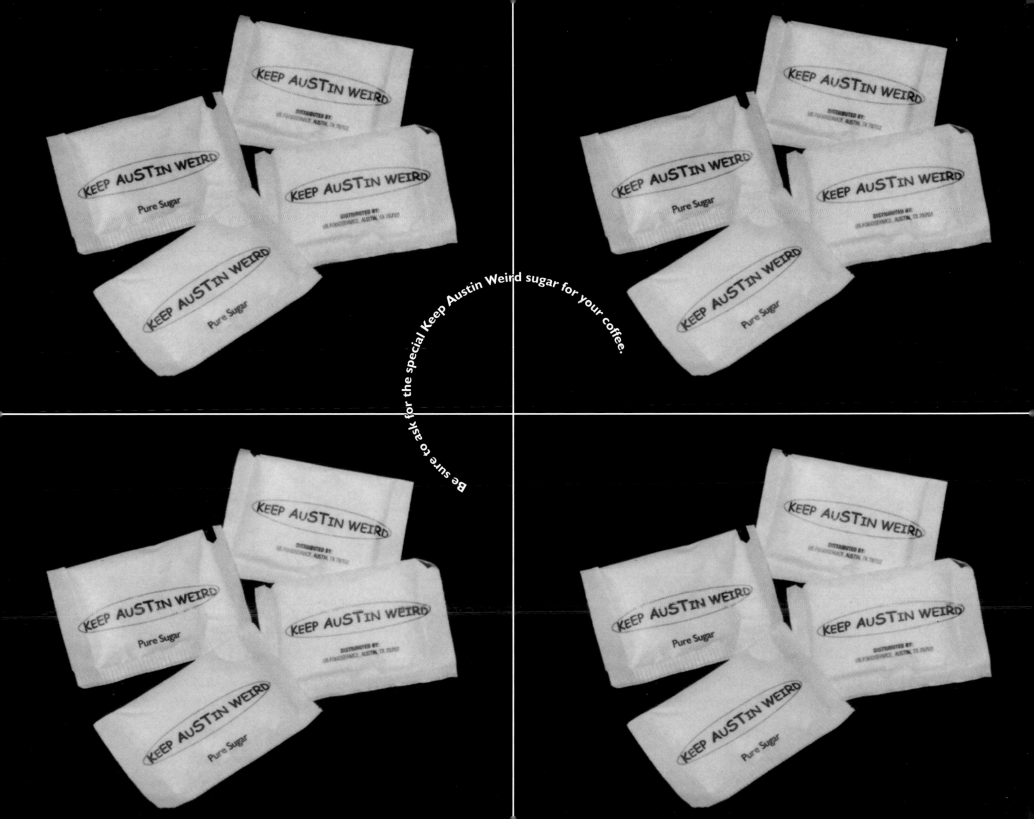

Be sure to ask for the special Keep Austin Weird sugar for your coffee.

Chapter 11
Unweird

Just as in every made-for-TV movie, there is an evil twin, a force that slithers within happily goofy Austin: a flip side of unweirdness. Whether it be bland conventionality or an aggressive Shiva-like destroyer, unweirdness must, sadly, be acknowledged.

Shocking news: Most of the unweirdness is tied to money. Whether it's tearing down Les Amis coffee shop to put up a Starbucks or tearing down half of the funky and historic Clarksville neighborhood to build MoPac freeway, follow the money.

Austin is blessed with an abundance of good restaurants, including a number of odd ones. But in the 1990s there was a sea change. High-end eateries became common as the dot-com boom boomed. Prices and pretension soared. In 2006, the bar at the Four Seasons Hotel proudly announced a $95 margarita. Visualize buying one and throwing it in the manager's face.

Here's an actual menu from one of the tonier restaurants:

SANS MAGIQUE

Starters

Blue Corn Smut with Vodka Hackberry Sauce
Mocha-Glazed Oxtail Pizza with Sun-Dried Mediterranean Gravel
Unborn Caviar and Flying Squirrel Roe
Chevre Rolet with a 386 Milled Head and Dual Carburetors
Braised Mixed Field Hands in Curdled Lhasa Apso Saliva
Soft Money Crabs in a White Wine Condescension
Mixed Greenbacks, with Krugerrand Croutons

Entrees

Free Range Poor People in Silly Hats Made of Arugula
Wild Baby Lamb Drowned in a Pith Helmet in Champagne Beet Sauce
Broken-Back Ribs, with Garnished Wages
Undraped Ordelon with Blue Potatoes Shaped Like Central American Dictators
Eel Tartare Stuffed, with Balsamic Waffles and Grits Drenched in Zinfandel Karo Syrup
Crisped Quail Beaks, with Twice-Chewed Baby Fennel Radicchio Endive Watercress Chicory Kale Escarole Swiss Chard Chutney
Sentient Veal in False Morel Raspberry Mint Sludge Served over Dried Wild Risotto with Saffron Porcini en Papillote
Sautéed Vegetarians, Assuaged with Guiltless Prevarications
Sirloin of Ancient Redwood Roasted over Redwood with Redwood Compote
Still-beating Heart of a Minimum-Wage Worker, with Fire-Roasted Bus Tokens and Resoled Shoe Leather

Desserts

Chocolate Incontinence
Lime Disease Sorbet
DentuCreme Brulee
Stuckey's Divinity in Durian Zest Marsala Custard
Assorted Currencies, with Gold-dusted Greenspan Dandruff

As the money pours into Austin, increasingly many smaller, character-filled houses in the central neighborhoods are being leveled and replaced with behemoths that often have massive garages as the prominent feature. ("A car lives here," as a friend put it.) It got so bad that in 2006 the city council passed the "McMansion" ordinance that limits the size of replacement houses in certain parts of town.

The lovely new style of Austin homes.

A local Mazda dealer, in May 2004, started offering a pickup truck with a "Keep Austin Weird" package. ("Free T-shirt with a test drive!") If only it really were a true weird Austin truck—the bed filled with burnt orange Jell-O, a water balloon cannon, strobe light headlamps...

"Make Austin Normal" is a painfully obvious reaction to KAW. They actually sell crap that says "I Love Big Box Stores" and "Buy from Chain Stores." Their website has a blog where the adamantly normal promote the glories of homogeneity. Similar spinoffs have happened in the bedroom suburbs, where there is a cry to "Keep Round Rock Normal." (Although, to the city's credit, someone spotted one saying "Keep Round Rock Pleasantly Unusual.") In the creatively challenged home of Texas A&M University you can get "Keep College Station Normal" T-shirts. The perfect gift for your rigid acquaintances.

Can we build a wall to prevent these people from immigrating to Austin (and also to keep out Californians who speculate on real estate but don't live here)?

A light traffic day on IH-35.

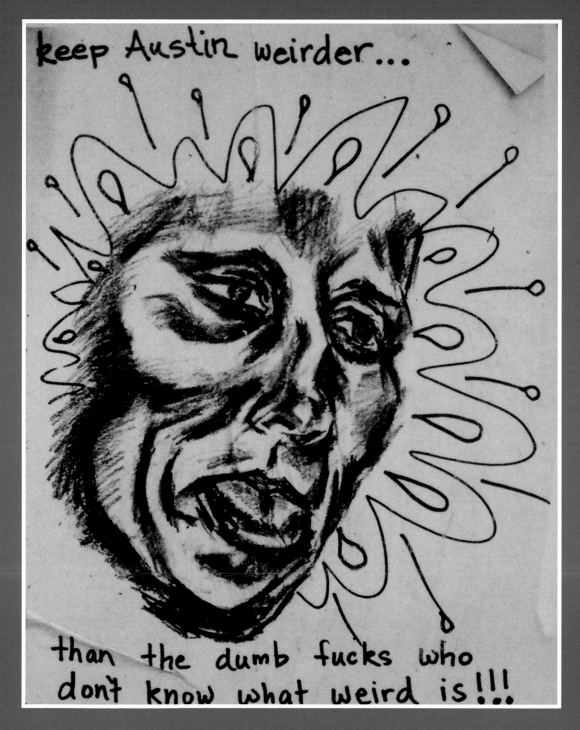

The weirder-than-thou crowd is a small but annoying aspect of unweirdness in Austin.

More Books on
Weird Austin and Texas

If you haven't had enough, here are some books that travel down paths similar to this one.

Friedman, Kinky. *The Great Psychedelic Armadillo Picnic: A "Walk" in Austin*. New York: Crown Journeys, 2004.

Kelso, John. *Texas Curiosities: Quirky Characters, Roadside Oddities, and Other Offbeat Stuff*. 2nd ed. Guilford, CN: Globe Pequot, 2004.

Loving, Vikki and Gregg Cestaro. *Wildly Austin: Austin's Landmark Art*. Austin: Wildly Austin, 2004.

Pohlen, Jerome. *Oddball Texas: A Guide to Some Really Strange Places*. Chicago: Chicago Review Press, 2006.

Treat, Wesley, Heather Shade, and Rob Riggs. *Weird Texas: Your Travel Guide to Texas's Best Kept Secrets*. New York: Sterling, 2005.